SELECTED POEMS *and* THE TESTAMENT

SELECTED POEMS

and

THE TESTAMENT

Alfred Williams

A FACSIMILE REPRINT

THE HOBNOB PRESS

Selected Poems was first published by Erskine MacDonald Ltd, London, in December 1925; 'The Testament' was first published in *Nature and Other Poems*, by Erskine MacDonald, London, in October 1912

This edition published in June 2020 by The Hobnob Press,
8 Lock Warehouse, Severn Road, Gloucester GL1 2GA
www.hobnobpress.co.uk

Preface and design © John Chandler, 2020

British Library Cataloguing in Publication Data
A catalogue record for this book is available from the British Library

ISBN 978-1-906978-86-0

Additional material typeset in Doves Type
Typesetting and origination by John Chandler

PREFACE

Centenaries offer a chance for reassessment and commemoration. This book, *The Selected Poems of Alfred Williams*, although not published until December 1925, was commissioned, planned and largely set up in type during the first half of 1920, a century ago as I write. It represents, in the words of Leonard Clark, his biographer, nearly all of Williams' poems worthy of preservation. 'The book will remain as a momument to his love of nature and mankind; it represents the positive creed of a man who, like the metaphysicals, completely achieved an escape of the spirit and who blended himself with something outside himself "which makes the new life a new creation".'

Alfred Williams was born of a Welsh father and a Wiltshire mother in 1877 in South Marston, a then remote village four miles east of Swindon – better known in recent years for its industrial estates and the gargantuan Honda car plant. His early life followed the trajectory of many adolescent boys in that part of Wiltshire: village schooling, farm labour for a pittance, then the enticement of better money 'inside' – as employment in Swindon railway works was generally known. Twenty-two years of heat and noise and a hammerman's strenuous labour broke his health, and in 1914, days after war began, he left the works for a life of poverty and barely successful market gardening in his home village, punctuated by inspirational military service in India. He died in 1930, still in his fifties, still excruciatingly poor, a few weeks before his first love, Mary Peck, whom he had married in 1903.

Not, on the face of it, a very successful life. But set that against his achievements. Self-taught proficiency in Latin, Greek and Sanskrit; author of six volumes of poems; chronicler in three prose books of country life, legend, nature and song; forthright reporter of the hardships of industrial labour; tireless folksong collector; prolific contributor to newspapers and magazines; fêted by the poet laureate and literary establishment of his day. And yet who now reads or remembers him, outside a small band of enthusiasts centred on his homeland of Swindon and the upper Thames valley? Few – which is a pity, because in his poetry and his depictions of rural life, he still has so much to offer, so much to enjoy.

In his lifetime Alfred Williams enjoyed the support and loyal friendship of those who recognised his worth. Lord Edmond Fitzmaurice, Liberal politician, cabinet minister, and scion of a noble Wiltshire landowning family, was one. Another was John Bailey, literary critic, man of letters and chairman of the National Trust. And a third was Reuben George, campaigning socialist mayor of Swindon and local hero. A fourth influence was the nature writer and novelist Richard Jefferies, known only through his books (he died when Alfred was ten), but an inspiring fellow-enthusiast for the same hills and vales of north Wiltshire. The two authors share a stone memorial on downland south of Swindon.

Selected Poems, the summation of Alfred's achievement as a poet, includes tributes in verse to Richard Jefferies ('The Earth Lover', pages 90-1) and Lord Fitzmaurice (page 169). It is prefaced by John Bailey's introduction, and dedicated, with permission, to the poet laureate, Robert Bridges. My copy, now a little foxed and discoloured, from which this facsimile edition is taken, is inscribed by Alfred and appears to have been given by him to Reuben George as a Christmas present in 1925. The book had been published on 16 December of that year (although the imprint says 1926), and it is pleasing to imagine the elation that these two close friends must have enjoyed as they examined the handsome volume together.

There is one poem, and one of Alfred's longest, which by rights should have been included in the selection but (presumably for reasons of space) was omitted. Entitled 'The Testament' it was published in 1912 in an earlier collection, and was received by critics with enthusiasm and acclamation. Written during repeated visits to a spot by the River Cole near his home, it is an extraordinary hymn to nature – a meditation and celebration, a summation of a remarkable man's philosophy of life. I have reprinted it as an appendix.

John Chandler
May 2020

For more information about Alfred Williams visit the website of the two organisations devoted to celebrating his life and works: the Alfred Williams Heritage Society and the Friends of Alfred Williams.

THE SELECTED POEMS
OF ALFRED WILLIAMS

THE SELECTED POEMS

OF

ALFRED WILLIAMS

rueben George Xmas 1925

WITH MUCH NEW AND RECENT WORK HITHERTO
UNPUBLISHED AND AN INTRODUCTION BY JOHN
BAILEY, M.A.

Alfred Williams

LONDON, W.C.1
ERSKINE MACDONALD LTD.

Printed in Great Britain
by Fox, Jones & Co., Kemp Hall Press, St. Aldate's, Oxford.

TO MY FRIEND
ROBERT BRIDGES

INTRODUCTION

My friend, Mr. Alfred Williams, has done me
the honour of asking me to write a few lines of
preface to this selection of his poems. I am glad
to find myself associated with him in this or any
other way. But I feel, and I am sure his readers
will agree with me, that no such preface is needed.
The majority of them will not now be making his
acquaintance for the first time. They will have
read some of his already published books, whether
of prose or verse, and they will know beforehand
what they have to look for—the thoughts and
feelings of an exceptionally honest, keen-eyed, and
tender-hearted man. And more than that. The
circumstances of his life, and his singular reaction
to them, have made Mr. Williams a rare and in-
teresting figure. Here is a man who passes from
a boyhood spent at a village school and in work on
a farm to years of exhausting labour in the heated
atmosphere of a railway forge. And yet before
middle life this man of little official education and,
apparently, less leisure, has taught himself French,
Latin, and Greek, and found time to acquire, in
addition to all that, a remarkable knowledge both
of the folklore and the natural history of his native
county.

Obviously such a man is no ordinary man. It

is true that Mr. Williams has had some exceptionally good fortune. He owes a great deal to the unwearying friendship and generosity of Lord Fitzmaurice, without whose assistance his first book might never have been published. But no help from outside can do more than give a man a chance of showing what he is worth. Lord Fitzmaurice could have done nothing for Mr. Williams if he had not possessed, what is so plainly proved by what he has done, an energy of mind and spirit which may fairly be called extraordinary. Experiences are for those who can find them. There are men (I have met one) who can go through such a catastrophe as the sinking of the *Titanic* and appear to have seen and felt nothing. There are also those who cannot walk along half a mile of ordinary road without experiencing many thoughts and feelings, many pleasures and sympathies which not only interest but even excite them. One has only to turn to the books that Mr. Williams has written to see which class he belongs to. Till the war he had scarcely left his native county: and yet his work at the forge, his life among his neighbours, his wanderings about his Wiltshire hills and woods and river-banks had given him more interesting experiences than are ever enjoyed by most of those who can rush at will from New York to Cairo, and from Cairo to Calcutta.

And then came the war, and after several rejections he got into the army as an artilleryman.

Here, too, he had practically to find his adventures: they did not come of their own accord. He was neither killed nor wounded, nor even taken prisoner. Indeed, with the exception of being in an exciting affair with submarines in the Bay of Biscay while outward bound for German East Africa, he was never in actual contact with the enemy, for in consequence of a gun accident in Ireland he missed the opportunity of the French battlefield. Similar ill-luck befell him afterwards in India, for while his battery was mobilizing for the Afghan front in 1919, he had the mortification of being taken to hospital with typhus. But still, he had the experience of his life. He did his soldiering well and was publicly complimented by his Commanding Officer as the best limber-gunner of his battery. While other soldiers, one suspects, slept, or idled away their leisure time, he was busy, facing heat and discomfort to get what acquaintance he could with the life, art, and religion of the natives of India. The result—or one result—is to be seen in the poems about India here published for the first time. On his return to England, finding himself without a home or employment, with the aid of his devoted wife and an old mason, he built a house, and, taking a plot of land, set about getting his living with the cultivation of fruits and vegetables. His love of Hindu literature now induced him to learn Sanskrit in order to read the famous Indian Epics and the Vedic Hymns in the original.

It is not the business of the writer of a preface to the poems of a living man to attempt anything like a critical estimate. That must come from others after the book has appeared. Here compliments would be an impertinence, criticism an intrusion. I will only venture to say one or two words. Bravery, sincerity, sympathy and intelligence do not by themselves make poetry. But they are the best foundation on which to build it. That they are all here in abundance will be clear to every reader. Mr. Williams's attitude towards life, as we see it everywhere in this book, plainly includes them all. It is the attitude which we get, for instance, in his little poem " Futurity " (which incidentally shows that he can write blank verse) :

> " Who walls his bosom up
> With burden of resolve, and ventureth
> To combat doubt with Faith's prerogative,
> Hath no more terror of what elements
> Waste the wide underworld than whoso walketh
> In summer meadows at high noon would fear
> Dark midnight, and the shades that usher it."

Courage is here the dominant note. But the others are all in the little poem, though perhaps more visible, or audible, elsewhere, as in some of the lyrics. Still more are they all, and other things too, present in those remarkable poems called "Natural Thoughts and Surmises " and " The Hills." There is, I think, nothing in the volume in which Mr. Williams so completely achieves that escape of the spirit which is poetry, that blending of a man's self with something outside him which makes the new life of a new creation. Let me quote the last section of " The Hills."

" Flow, endless rivers of thoughts and imaginings, flow !
And blow, you ministering, murmuring breaths of the breezes, blow !
Over the ultimate hills and marginal blue of the plain,
Bending the passionate, reasoning blooms, and the stalks of the grain,
Sifting the innermost soul of the woods, and thoughts of the leaves,
Looping and twining your manifold arms round the gold of the sheaves,
Blow softly, faintly, strongly out of the sea,
And blow the healing breath of the hills in the valley to me !
I know, somewhere in my heart, that a thousand enemies wait
To rend my quivering soul, but I fear not invisible Fate,
Rapt with the calm, cool, sensible breath that distils
The clarified, purified, sisterly soul of the hills ;
And I look in the glass of my heart, and hourly abide you,
In the long, low evergreen valley that stretches beside you.
O never shall the flattering cheer of the crowd, the chink of the gold,
The pride of station and wealth be glittering fetters to hold
The scathless soul of the seer from the beauty that fills
The far, sweet visage of space, and the heart of the hills ;
But ever while journeying wheels revolve in the race to be run,
So shall my heart beat true to the woods, and the hills, and the sun."

There are obvious influences at work here ; and the influence of Whitman is even more obvious in " Natural Thoughts and Surmises." But Mr. Williams is no mere echo of Whitman, or Meredith, or anybody else. He is himself. Only, like all wise poets, and, most of all, the wisest and the greatest, he has openly, unashamedly, gone to school with his great predecessors. He has not, like some of his contemporaries, made the mistake of supposing that a poet can handle his art as if there had been such a thing in the world as a poet before. He knows that all art is based on a tradition, building on which it tries to make something which is at once old and new.

That takes me to my final word. There has grown up in the past hundred years, with the greater seriousness of poetry, a notion that there is no room for any but the supreme poets. Mr. Williams would be the last to lay claim to be one of these. But no such notion as that existed in the eighteenth century, or the seventeenth, or the sixteenth. And the truth is that there are times when we can read Cowper but are not up to Milton. Indeed, there were hundreds of Cowper's contemporary readers who owed to him the opening of their eyes to poetry, while to Milton they never owed, nor perhaps could have owed, anything at all. Often, in fact, if they ever came to love Milton it was due to Cowper, who showed them the way. So do not let us make the short-sighted and insolent mistake of writing poets off our list because there

xii

are greater men on it. I do not know whether Mr. Williams has been a reader of Cowper. But some of his poems—such as " In My Garden," in one way, and " India " in another—have recalled Cowper to me. I am sure Cowper would have loved and praised their simplicity, sincerity, and quiet beauty, the ever-ready sympathy of their poet's heart, and the ever-watchful curiosity with which he notes the ways of nature and of man. ᐧ And if we are wise, so may we. We live in a time of great expectations and great disappointments. There is no help or hope for us in the pessimists who live in a past which cannot return. And sometimes there seems to be even less in the confident and loud-tongued " Futurists " of all sorts whose " future " often seems less inviting than any known past. This book shows us a man who, though the opposite of a favoured child of fortune, has known how to live in the present and find in it abundance of things interesting and beautiful, lovable and good. We may easily do worse than go to school with him. That we have the opportunity of doing through his poems.

JOHN BAILEY.

CONTENTS

III

NATURE POEMS

IV

INDIAN POEMS

V
VARIOUS POEMS

VI
SONNETS

NOTE

THE " Cuckoo Song " has been sung by Madame Melba ; music by Mr. Roger Quilter. Of the " Love Lyrics," several were first printed in *The Westminster Gazette*, and *The Outlook*. " India," and " East and West " were published in *The Empress* (Calcutta), and the majority of the other Indian lyrics appeared in *The Englishman* (Calcutta), or *The Indian Daily Telegraph* (Lucknow), while the author was on military service in India as a gunner in the R.G.A. The sonnets on Stonehenge were originally printed in *The Salisbury Times*. I acknowledge my indebtedness to the Editors for permission to reproduce the pieces. Several of the longer poems taken from the earlier books have been slightly curtailed to allow of their inclusion in the volume.

A. W.

Corrigendum.
Read " holds " for " hold," l. 4, p. 89.

I.

EARLY POEMS.

CUCKOO SONG.

Blow, blow, winds of May,
Ruffle the bloomy spray,
Blow all the balm away;
Hark! 'tis my roundelay.
    Cuckoo! Cuckoo!

Here's to the merry morn,
Another joy is born,
Hail to the huntsman's horn,
For the bluebell greets the corn.
    Cuckoo! Cuckoo!

Long ere the oak-leaves shine,
Or the woolly buds on the vine
Promise the blood of the wine,
I dream of the dear confine,
Of the woods that are mine, that are mine.
    Cuckoo! Cuckoo!

With iron frost on the bark,
And the hazels stiffened and stark,
Far from the doom of the dark
I drown the lay of the lark.
    Cuckoo! Cuckoo!

I have neither sorrow nor strife,
Music's the joy of my life,
Beauty and pleasure are rife,
And all the world is my wife.
    Cuckoo! Cuckoo!

Now burns the planet on high,
And melts the crown of the sky,
The flowers wither and die;
O, open, my sail-wings, and fly
Where bushels of almond-bloom lie.
  Cuckoo! Cuckoo!

THE BLACKBIRD'S SONG.

MARGUERITE!

'Tis pleasant in the balmy woods to meet
After the silent snow and bitter sleet,
To feel the gentle warmth, the soothing heat,
And sitting on this bough is something sweet;
  Marguerite!

Marguerite!

'Tis long since the rounded acorns beat
A way through the leaves to the mossy-sweet
And scented patch far under our feet,
And the reaper slew the gold of the wheat;
  Marguerite!

Marguerite!

In winter time, when the winds are fleet
And the earth is wound with a blinding sheet
An ivy-bough is my sheltered seat,
Water my wine and berries my meat,
But I guard my song till the springing heat;
  Marguerite!

6

Marguerite!
My heart will burst if I do not greet
My blue-eyed bird with her singing sweet.
Now the red-breast loiters and swallows fleet,
The neighbour lark sings over the wheat,
Bluebells tinkle and lambkins bleat;
                Marguerite!

                Marguerite!
A brook I know, where the minnows meet
To swim and glide in the glassy sheet,
And O! the water is sweet, so sweet,
And thither I go in the dust and the heat
And drink my fill in the cool retreat
While the sun streams down on the burning peat;
                Marguerite!

                Marguerite!
I sing from my soul, for my song will beat
As a hundred hoofs, when the hunters meet
To chase the thief from his woody seat;
I sing to the blossoms, and sing to the wheat,
In shadow and light, in shower and heat,
But most to myself, for singing is sweet;
                Marguerite!

7

PHILIP SPARROW

THE linnet is nigh,
The lark's in the sky,
And singing and ringing
Are all the woods by.
  Philip! Philip!

All night, in the eaves,
I dream of the sheaves,
There's dew on the grasses
And bloom on the leaves.
  Philip! Philip!

I know when the spring
Has ruffled her wing
By the joy in my soul;
Then louder I sing
  Philip! Philip!

The snow and the rain
Have beaten in vain,
There'll be bushels of berries
And acres of grain.
  Philip! Philip!

The thistle and reed
Both bloom to my need,
Earth stores to my harvest
And scatters my seed.
  Philip! Philip!

8

Thus, though I am least
Of man and of beast,
Though poor in my state
I've enough, and a feast.
    Philip! Philip!

THE ROOK'S MONODY.

WHAT troubles have I?
The woods and the sky,
The wold and the weald
Are my kingdom, my field.
I am lord, I am king
Of winter and spring,
Of autumn and summer,
And every new-comer
Attends when I sing, when I sing.
The birds of the woodland bow down to my law,
The hawk, and the kestrel, the eagle, and daw.
    Caw! Caw! Caw!

Behold, how I shine!
All glory is mine,
All colour and glitter
Of beauty — and better —
I treasure and take
To my breast, to my back,
In folds and in tangles
Of rays and of spangles,
And smoothness of velvety black.

9

In summer and harvest, in frost and in thaw
Earth scatters and litters some food for my maw.
    Caw! Caw! Caw!

My voice is as sweet
As the milk of the wheat,
And plainer and purer,
And richer and surer,
Than all the wild thrushes
That bawl in the bushes,
Both musical, mellow, and meet;
For, when I am near
In the spring of the year,
And warble both over and under,
For envy all cease,
The valleys have peace,
And nature is struck with a wonder;
All suffer my praises and sing to my law,
The linnets, and thrushes, the dove, and the daw.
    Caw! Caw! Caw!

What though I am scorned,
And hunted and horned
From bushes and bowers,
And tree-tops and towers,
And banned for a season
From right and from reason,
And warred on with pilfering powers!
Thus monarchs must suffer
For smoother or rougher,
And gather some thorns with their flowers.

Howbeit the swain
Still scatters me grain,
And heralds my note with a flourish,
And, while my compeers
Want berries and ears,
I fatten and feed till they perish.
In summer, and autumn, in frost, and in thaw,
Earth scatters and litters some food for my maw,
For I am the king, and all else is my law.
     Caw! Caw! Caw!

THE REAPER'S SONG.

The tufted lark is over the plain,
  And the southern breezes blow,
The dew-balm's wet on the bending grain,
  Cheerily, merrily O!
The panting horses of the day
  Leap into the eastern sky,
Now 'tis time to be up and away,
  My nut-brown lass and I.

Sometimes within the hazel shade,
  At the point of noon or so,
I linger with my nut-brown maid,
  Cheerily, merrily O!
While the poppies droop and wither,
  And the sun smokes on the plain,
Then I and my lass together
  Go into the wheat again.

11

The scarlet poppy, tricked and drest,
  Is a lovely feast, I know;
But my lass is featured like the West,
  Cheerily, merrily O!
Her beauty is a stainless glass,
  Her faith too strong to tell,
The glories of the hour will pass
  But her's eternal dwell.

Bring out the bonny, wholesome ale,
  And let the river flow,
The tipsy sun hangs over the dale,
  Cheerily, merrily O!
The blue-bell and the honey-leaf,
  The poppy and the grain,
Are gathered in the scented sheaf
  And die upon the plain.

THE HARVEST SONG.

MAKE haste, you reapers, one and all,
  True merry souls we'll be,
The shepherd and the woodman call,
  And Meg and Marjorie;
Bring out the whistle and the reed,
  The posy and the crown,
And trip it on the level mead
  Ere the jolly sun goes down.

There's Stella, and Bella,
  And Bess, and Priscilla,
And Daisy, and Lily,
  There's Tom, and there's Willie,
And all the young fools of the town.

Bring roses some, and hazel nuts,
  And leaves and berries all,
And russets from the bough that juts
  High over the western wall;
And brave queen-apples, rosy-ripe,
  The fittest for a crown,
And wildings with the ruddy stripe
  Ere the jolly sun goes down.

Call forth the lordly wassail-bowl
  That raises to divine,
Crowned with the purple-streaming soul
  Of the blood-red harvest wine;
There's one gate leads to sorrow,
  And another to renown,
But 'tis long until to-morrow
  When the jolly sun is down.

LIDDINGTON HILL.

The friendship of a hill I know,
  Above the rising down,
Where the balmy southern breezes blow,
  But a mile or two from town;

The budded broom and heather
  Are wedded on its breast,
And I love to wander thither
  When the sun is in the west.

As birds within the woodland walk,
  In the early morning hour,
Our childish tongues begin to talk,
  Above the high hill-tower;
Ere the woodman leaves his shelter,
  Or the shepherd seeks his fold,
While the woolly conies skelter
  Along the coltsfoot gold.

No other monument hast thou
  To point the hills around,
But the crescent scar upon thy brow
  Of the bloody battle-mound:
A hundred squares and hollows
  Close-gather at thy feet,
With clovers and with fallows,
  And the golden-bearded wheat.

A thousand years will come and go,
  And thousands more will rise,
My buried bones to dust will grow,
  And dust defile my eyes;
But when the lark sings o'er the wold,
  And the swallow weaves her nest,
My soul will take the coltsfoot gold
  And blossom on thy breast.

14

THE SHEPHERD'S SONG.

Sleep close, my pretty lambs, so warm and white,
The breeze is gentle and the moon is light;
The god of folds, my sheep, your peace ensure,
The hill is vacant and the pen secure.

No nightly prowling thieves the wood invade,
Or midnight monster casts a creeping shade,
Slow round the shadows to the meadow lawn,
And vanish with the purple dusk of dawn.

Now close the sleepy buds upon the tree,
The flowers yield no more sweetness to the bee,
The drowsy beetle winds his native horn,
And loudly bellows through the bursting thorn.

The blustering breezes have unlocked the year,
A hundred various hues and dyes appear;
To-day I loitered where the lily blows,
And prickly buds proclaim the nestling rose.

To-morrow, if our guardian heaven approve,
And no stout tempest ruffle in the grove,
Where blooming hawthorn scatters from the tree,
There you shall wander with my herds and me,

While from the topmost height the heat descends,
And o'er the pool the gentle lily bends;
Till Evening dons her robe of rosy-gold,
And purple twilight nestles o'er the fold.

15

THE BLACKBIRD'S CANTICLE.

O ʜᴏᴡ the bonny blackbird sang,
On the twisted old thorn bough!
Now the hollow meadow-valleys hang
In a trance to listen, "'Tis young, young, youɪ
The morning, morning," sang the blackbird.
"I saw the shepherd, the old shepherd,
Going slow, very slow,
Down the bend of the hill,
And around him, around him,
So playful and gentle,
No bigger than our nestlings
New-hatched in the thorn-bush,
A hundred frisking and frolicing
Wee things like May-blossoms.
And one, more beautiful,
More rounded and purely delicate,
White as the whitest snow-drift
That piles the hedges in winter,
And sweeter than the pure May-lily,
Or loveliest of lovely bean-blossoms,
He was carrying, carrying,
Like a rose on his bosom,
As we carry the crimson currants,
Or sweet luscious strawberries,
New-gathered from the garden,
To our home in the tufted apple-tree."

"And I heard the low wind whisper
Balmy through the thicket of the maple
To the modest blue-eyed violet,

16

More sweetly and exquisitely scented
Than the rosy-tinted cups of hawthorn,
That a lovely lover would come to her,
More palely beautiful than Narcissus,
And with divinely rapturous ecstasies,
And beauty-breathing, odorous syllables
Of soul-compelling and victorious love,
Reward her long-hid jewelled modesty
With joys undreamt of".

                              "Cher-a-peeke!
Peeke! peeke! peeke!" sang the blackbird,
"All honour to the daisy, the daisy,
The pale-green, yellow-hearted primrose,
The blowing plumes of the crimson herb-sorrel,
Ruddy oak leaves, and crowns of poplar,
And the smooth-leaved, smooth-rinded beeches;
All the green-souled, green-tinted,
Gold-leaved, and purple-mantled,
Impearled and imbrasured jewelry
Of the bordered meadow and running streamlet.
And to my rival minstrel, the dewy skylark,
Blithe-rippling, and attunéd like a fountain,
Rising in the shadowy and shadow-less morning;
And the clear-voiced, mellifluous song-thrushes,
Answering the pierced and stricken nightingale,
Sweet-souled, sweet-piteous, moving tremulous
Immeasurably harmonious utterances
To the dream-inspiring pale-orbed visionary".

"And you, sweet, tender-hearted choristers,
. Pure, unaffected, piping, tell-tale linnets,
By rose, or briar, or clinging honey-suckle;

17

Also the tricked and conscious bullfinch,
Sitting on bough like eastern Emperor,
With coloured and brocaded ornamenture
Of corseleted and pinioned imagery,
Dropping sweet pearls of silver minstrelsy
On the redolent gems beneath".

          "And then the red-breast,
So faintly and sweetly querulous,
Tuning all day in the little thorn thicket,
Or hopping in and out of the ever-green
And berried privet, or in the cattle stall,
Soothing the cowherd with an amorous ditty.
And the strong-eyed, vocal wood-pigeon,
Sitting on oak, or duly embowered
In the branching elm, or on the drooping
And graceful curvature of the nervous ash-stature,
Or the giant-limbed, all-powerful beeches,
With her friendly conversant and sister tenant
The gentle turtle-dove, soft, tremulous,
Brooding on nameless griefs and lovely sorrows,
Dreams of discarded, unrequited lovings,
And shadowy wrongs and treasons uncommitted." ·

"Next the blue-feathered and soft-tinted starling,
That loves the old ram's back, and the woolly heifer,
Companions of the meadow, with the garrulous
White-throated and white-breasted swifts, the strangers,
New landed from the straits. Honour, all honour,
Honour, honour," sang the blackbird,
While the celestial-canopied, life-giving planet
Serenely rose above the piney ramparts
And empire of the pillared, turreted East.

ROSALIND.

ROSALIND! Rosalind!
Noble-hearted, rich, refined
In all madness of the mind,
Heedless as the frolic wind,
Swift to break, and slow to bind,
Are you not unkind, unkind,
    Rosalind? Rosalind?

Rosalind! Rosalind!
Pre-appointed, pre-designed
The eclipse and envy of your kind,
Warmth of passion, wealth of mind,
Beauty, wisdom, wit combined,
Must I die, resolved, resigned,
Dying thus your faith to find,
    Rosalind? Rosalind?

Rosalind! Rosalind!
Richly sighted, poorly blind,
Fickle as the changing wind,
O beware! lest, while you sing,
Dying, I revive and spring,
Fix you with a deadly sting,
That you fall, conserved, consigned
To a fate beyond your kind,
    Rosalind! Rosalind!

19

DAPHNIS.

LEAVE thy flocks for a spell
On the slope of the fell
To wander together,
Make haste to come hither,
I've a burning secret to tell.

Here's a fern for thy seat,
And a pause from the heat,
With garlands and dresses,
And leaves for thy tresses,
And strawberry crowns for thy feet.

The bull and the ram
Will care for the dam;
The sun's in the stubble,
Your flocks are no trouble,
And cool is the shade where I am.

Alone let us lie
To live and to die,
And dying and living,
With joy past the giving,
We'll drain the sweet cup till 'tis dry.

Come early, come soon,
'Tis the death of the noon,
And through the cloud-curtain,
All dim and uncertain,
I see the young horns of the moon.

20

THE KEEPER'S DAUGHTER.

WITHIN my garden blooms a rose,
  Sweet-blooded as the soul that wrought her;
But poorly her perfection shows
  Matched with fair Kate, the keeper's daughter.

I met her first amid the corn,
  Rich with the dust of golden slaughter,
Where Plenty wreathes his winding horn,
  Sweet-blushing Kate, the keeper's daughter.

A wreath of poppies for her hair,
  And berries from the bush I brought her,
Creation lightened unaware
  Around the keeper's matchless daughter.

The richest heritage of kings,
  Wealth of two worlds, had never bought her,
And wisdom unto beauty springs
  Ennobling Kate, the keeper's daughter.

Soon at the village church we'll wed,
  And live the vows my love has taught her;
Eternity shall bow my head
  Ere I spurn Kate, the keeper's daughter.

JULIA AND MARGARET.

SWEET Julia and Margaret
  On a merry summer's day,
In a sunny meadow-garden met
  To roll among the hay.

A little distance, by the wood,
  A cunning she-wolf lay,
Her greedy eyes were red as blood,
  For she saw the lambkins stray.

The fiery furnace of the sun
  Beguiled the lambs at play,
Till they sank and slumbered, one by one,
  In the shade of the high noon-day;

Fie Julia! Fie Margaret!
  What would the shepherd say,
The roses and the lilies met,
  And the lambs so far away?

So the wolf up-flew with a whooping yell
  Beneath the hawthorn spray,
While the lily maidens rose and fell
  On the billows of the hay.

At even, when the shepherd came,
  At the setting of the ray,
Around him, like a purple flame,
  The blood-stained heather lay.

But Julia and Margaret,
  The gayest of the gay,
Still tumbled, though the dew was wet
  On the balm-leaf of the hay.

SONG.

(From an unpublished Play, "Sardanapalus")

ALAS! and woe!
How fleet the summers come! How fast the winters go!
The day-star, labouring from the East,
The waters on the troubled shore
Soon, soon will cease their muffled roar,
Soon, soon will turn into the West,
The winds will seek the mountain-crest
Till the fair Morn awakes more blithely than before.

The merchant toiling in the deep,
The patient ox, the cheerful swain,
Will turn unto their homes again,
Will their appointed slumbers keep ;
Kings only are bereft of sleep
That chase the god away with their lascivious train.

Love sits upon the warrior's crest,
And pricks him on to fearful deeds ;
An envious jealousy proceeds
Even from the woful shepherd's breast ;
But kings deride that dainty feast,
And crown the rosy hours with dark and fulsome weeds.

23

Alas! and woe!
The streams are black with rain! the hills are
     white with snow!
No cheerful pipe, no sounding flute
Is heard within the shepherd's grove,
The time is past for blissful love,
And every several bird is mute;
Now Winter pleads his raging suit
With drifting Earth beneath, and towering
     Heaven above.

AMARYLLIS.

AMARYLLIS! Amaryllis!
Dearest daughter of the plain,
Lovelier than the arch-eyed Phyllis,
Wildings, buttercups, and lilies,
Will you kill me with disdain,
    Amaryllis?

Woolly flocks, as soft as snow,
Whiten all the steppes below;
Bleating goats, as fully white,
Climb the rock's tremendous height;
Yet I take no dear delight,
    Amaryllis.

Roses, ruddy as the morn,
Open on the scented thorn;
Nature tunes her lightest lay,
Nature's breath is sweet with may,
Nothing pleases, thou away,
    Amaryllis.

24

A milky goat I will provide,
A milky kid on either side,
In richest pastures newly-fed,
With flowery chains and garlands led,
And ivy-chaplets for thy head,
    Amaryllis.

Ah! she turns, she flees away,
Laughing at my simple lay;
Gifts, I see, are fond and frail,
Only force and fraud prevail.
Some such arts I will employ,
Love is taken with a toy,
    Amaryllis.

ON THE DOWNS.

O MY heart! the day has been
  Full of bitter. Here we rest,
Unobtruding and unseen;
Stretched upon the shaded green,
  Unpossessing, unpossest
With the burning scorn of anger,
Yielding to divinest languor,
  Dream we on the magic West.

Higher now ascend, and higher!
  We must rise, as one in one
Worlds are kindled, stars aspire;
Thus we come to our desire:

25

Now the glory of the sun
In many a spangled, starry crescent,
Over hill and dale quiescent
  Fades at length; the day is done.

What if soul and body parted
  For a minute or an hour,
If the spirit death-ward darted,
Torn asunder, mocked, and thwarted
  By a universal power;
Would the body re-inherit
Heart, and soul, and mind, and spirit,
  Would the sweet survive the flower?

O the bonny hills of heather!
  O the upland and the wold!
Sunshine under darkest weather,
Drawing heart and heart together,
  Marvellous and manifold;
Scented bean, and clinging clover,
Purple-tinted, rubied over
  With the sunset, cloth of gold.

Here we lie, a single, double,
  One in married mood and mind;
Life at best is toil and trouble,
Honour but an empty bubble,
  Fame as fickle as the wind;
Death is sleep, a rising, setting,
A remembering and forgetting,
  Undefining, undefined.

Could we reap, in crowded places,
  Knowledge of a full delight,
While Imagination traces
In an endless sea of faces
  Beauty's hatred, Nature's spite?
O the thronging and the pressing,
And the madness of possessing,
  Forcing Freedom, wrenching Right!

What could stem the fateful forces
  Of Creation's law sublime,
Or prevent the Will that courses
With eternal, rich resources
  Steadfast as the trend of Time?
Could the word of change be spoken,
Or the wheel of fate be broken
  By one feeble poet's rhyme?

Break! you fetters that encumber
  Thought, that travails in the soul;
Thought! put off the scales of slumber,
Conquer distance, measure, number,
  Scorn the part, obtain the whole;
Knowledge fails, and Reason falters,
Wisdom waits, Affection alters,
  Only Hope attains the goal.

Much is writ, but more remaineth;
  Worlds are sought, but never won;
Weakness wills, and seldom gaineth,
Hoping most it least obtaineth;

27

Less is ended than begun;
Many sleep, but few awaken;
Much is lost, and little taken;
  Much attempted, little done.

Now the scented breezes, flowing
  From the bosom of the hill,
Set the cotton-grasses blowing,
And the little wood is glowing
  Sweetly silent, softly still;
North and West and South are holden
With a glory crimson-golden,
  Woof of rose and daffodil.

Hasten, heart! an end to dreaming!
  Thought, surcease! the hour is old;
Fainter now the West is gleaming,
Rosy still, but fainter seeming,
  Purple creeps into the gold;
And the blue-grey hills are dimmer,
And the twilights dance and glimmer
  On the rounding of the wold.

O for ever thus to mingle,
  One in spirit and in mood,
With the darling down and dingle,
While my pulses tremble, tingle
  With the teaching of my blood!
Still to find, and still to follow
Joy in every hill and hollow,
  Company in solitude.

Here is health and true devotion,
  All my want and all my need,
Riches vaster than the ocean,
Beauty, perfect rest, and motion,
  Balmy blossom, scented reed;
Nature's bonded mystic union,
And a deathless, dear communion
  With the world's immortal seed.

THE POET.

OF peopled worlds, and mighty-clashing kings,
  Thrones, empires, dynasties, the living dead,
The gold-harped prophet-seer and poet sings;
  All praise be on his head.

The Chian and the Mantuan bard remain
  Eternal as the hills; to Aeneas one,
To gods and heroes the other tuned his strain,
  Jove and his highest son.

Swift Pindar, rivalling the mountain-flood
  Down-thundering furious to the crested sea;
And sweet Alceus, cunning as a god
  In music's majesty.

Divine Orpheus, whose exalted strain
  Could sooth the savage breast; and she whose lyre,
The Lesbian songstress, animates the brain
  With never-quenching fire.

29

Next Roman Horace, and the bard of fate,
   Ovidius, richest in the vein of thought
And flooded fancy, whom the poet's state
   To branded exile brought;

Such was thy sovran will, and such thy frown,
   Immortal Caesar! whose embellished name
The thunder-peals of Time will echo down
   The thunder-hills of fame.

Soon Albion's bards arose, a mighty line,
   Our sturdy Chaucer first, the poet-sire
Of generous generations, true, divine,
   A chieftain of the lyre;

Whence that clear swan of Avon, Fancy's child,
   And learned Spenser, Mulla's minstrel long,
Sweet, pastoral Sidney, faithful Fletcher mild,
   And many a starry song

Sung in the tapestried, embroidered walls
   Of hoary mansions, with the Muses' breath,
Or in the canopied, emblazoned halls,
   Of good Elizabeth.

Last of the towering choir rose he who sung
   Of Eden's promises, and Eden's fruit,
Prophetic Milton, whose seraphic tongue
   Pronounced his rivals mute,

Whom countless constellations follow on,
   Fluting their carol notes from sea to sea,
Illustrious Wordsworth, sweet-voiced Tennyson,
   And hundreds more to be.

Mine is the common palm, yet would I bring
    One thankless offering to the Muses' shrine,
For, though the strain be feeble that I sing,
    The purpose is divine.

THE BROOK.

Flow on! happy stream,
    To the shining river;
We are as a dream,
    Thou wilt glide for ever;
Where the white stones gleam,
    And the pale leaves quiver,
Flow! thou happy stream,
    To the shining river.

Past the dewy mead,
    By the drooping willow,
Hurry o'er thy bed
    To the restless billow;
Where the sea-birds ride,
    And the dark waves sorrow,
Swinging with the tide
    May'st thou be to-morrow!

Lonely is the wood,
    Lonely is the hollow,
Spacious is the flood,
    Thither we must follow;
Soon our lives are sped
    Like the mountain heather,
Throng we to our bed
    With the leaves that wither.

31

THE GREEK PEASANT'S PRAYER FOR RAIN.

Rain! gentle Zeus, o'er the earth below,
  Quicken the fainting fields, and on the plain,
Where every herb and flower have ceased to grow,
  Scatter thy liquid sweets and smile again.

Lo! in the deepest dell, and where the glade
  Woke to the music of a prattling rill,
Is nought but mournful melancholy made,
  For the wild minstrels of the wood are still.

Now sicken the lean kine beneath the noon,
  And perish the young lambs within the fold,
Even the starry midnight and the moon
  Offer no comfort to us as of old;

But from the rising of the daily sun,
  When in the mocking heaven he first appears,
Till his late journey is complete and done,
  And night is past again and morning nears,

Labours the stricken earth as one oppressed,
  And spoiled and vanquished with a tyrant's power,
Hiding her frightened children on her breast
  And trembling at the passage of each hour.

Rain! gentle Zeus, scatter thy sweet showers
  Over the burning fields and o'er the plain,
Kindle still Nature with thy living powers
  And make the merry streamlets run again.

Then, when the distant hills and valleys shine
  And glisten with their gifts of yearly gold,
Thee will we worship with the rarest wine,
  And all the fairest favours of the fold.

FUTURITY.

WASTE not the troubled hours in summoning
Dreams from the sullen silence. What is, is.
What hath been, hath been. Dim Futurity,
Though wooed by many suitors, yieldeth not
Her caverned secrets, but still folds them up,
And draws her mystical and hooded garment
For ever fast about her, till high Death
With his tranced wand unbinds it. Perfect trust,
Obedience to the Will, sincerity,
White-handed Hope and close-grained Fellowship,
With spotless, stainless, pure virginity,
These will avail. Who walls his bosom up
With burden of resolve, and ventureth
To combat doubt with Faith's prerogative,
Hath no more terror of what elements
Waste the wide underworld than whoso walketh
In summer meadows at high noon would fear
Dark midnight, and the shades that usher it.

A WOMAN'S FACE.

TEACH me this happiness, to know
One bloom, one beauty, and one grace,
Ere sightless to the vast I go —
    A woman's face.

Earth harbours many treasures—gold,
Pearl, rubies, emeralds; and yet
One feature of the perfect mould
    Would pay the debt.

Nature, excelling as she goes,
Nor deeming aught conceived amiss,
First tried conclusions with the rose,
    Then gave us this,

In which perfections meet, as hue,
All sweetness, full, and unexprest;
Then, wanting further means, withdrew
    And dreamt the rest.

ODE TO SPRING.

Now lovely Nature, laughing-eyed,
Puts on her beauty and her pride,
A rosy radiant, beaming bride.
A belt of green with golden studs,
And bursting blossoms, bursting buds.
The scented foliage of her hair
Soft, gentle puffing Zephyrs bear.

34

The honey-sweetness of her mouth,
The full ambrosia of the South;
The gentle blood within her veins,
Are precious dews, and precious rains.
The rosy-tinted hawthorn white,
The bluebell, ringing with delight,
The daisy lettered on the lea,
The starry-pale anemone,
Deep violets, hidden in their beds,
And richest purples, richest reds,
Enkindled with the stealing heat,
Break into beauty at her feet.
New verdure greens the tufted pines,
New juices stir the pulsing vines,
Her living breath adorns the hill,
Her footstep prints the daffodil.
Azure the wonder of her eyes,
Her smile immortal as the skies,
And when she frowns above the copse
Her liquid soul dissolves in drops.
Pleased with the garment Beauty wears,
The rosy-sylvan Nymph appears,
And naked Graces, nightly seen
Sporting on the tufted green.
Immortal Hebe leads the dance,
And round the merry ring they prance,
With choral pomp and mirth the hours employ,
And crown the victors with a wreath of joy.

LINES ON A SUICIDE.

God rest thee! and have mercy for thy frailness,
And hold thee in His memory. Many fall
That more may prosper by the settlement,
As arms before a city are built up
By others' ruin. So thy destiny
Will be writ down to many, who shall name thee
Their most unhappy counsellor. I knew thee
When thou wert sinless; sinless I. The world
Moved to a harmony and wronged us not,
And life was silken-sailed. Suspicion
Of latter change ne'er crossed us, and together
Hourly we grew, as young and tender blossoms
Upon the self-same stem; laughed, wept, and sang.
Now cleaved we fast together at the school,
Now topped the branching elm; together mixed
In childish sports and pastimes, wandering
In dewy meadows under trees, for ever
Weaving fresh flowers in simplicity.
And I remember, as 'twere yesterday,
The windows of thy eyes full for thy mother,
And red with weeping, knowing not that sorrow
Is parcel of this dowry, a spun thread,
Deep-woven with Life's garment. Nurtured thus,
Yet following diverse fates instinctively,
As floods wave outward to the dropping moon,
We grew asunder. In thy sails a tempest
Blew with strange fury, but my bark swam on
O'er sunlight-stricken waters and strown calms,
Slower, but safer. Swift and sure thy fall was,

Whereat the angels weep; but God, in mercy,
For so He sent His Mediator down
To sit in judgment upon men, will hold
Uneven balance, counting evil weakness,
And only mourning that the good He gave thee
Were swallowed up in this mortality.

II.

LOVE LYRICS.

THE FINDING.

SWEET, and I have found thee!
Whither art thou fled,
With the garlands around thee
Wherewith thou hast bound thee,
And the dawn-light on thy head;
Eyes and lips meekly beseeching,
Love's language teaching?

As the East, that whitens
O'er the piney crest
Of the hills, and lightens,
So thy beauty brightens,
And the heart leaps in my breast;
As the rose, when it awaketh,
New sweetness taketh.

Love is never holden,
But away he slips,
Seeking to embolden,
Hiding in the golden
Snare of speaking lips;
But my heart, that beauty readeth,
No more sweet needeth.

THE TYPE.

ALL that in Nature's
Fairest to see
God, in the making,
Imaged in thee.

Blue of the mountain,
Silent and wise,
Azure of ocean,
Brightness of skies;

Soul of the violet,
The rose's hue,
Fragrance of lilies,
Sweetness of dew;

And, to conclude thee —
The fairest part —
Set his bright angel,
Love, in thy heart,

Where he sits ruling
In gentle guise,
With the sweet wisdom
Of lips and eyes.

IF SHE BE NEAR.

I CANNOT read, if she be near,
For O, mine eyes will lose the place,
And seek her out, to study there
The flower-like beauty of her face.

I cannot think, if she be near,
For O, the thought within me dies,
And all my wisdom is, to share
The deep-veiled mysteries of her eyes.

I cannot sleep, if she be near,
For O, the honey-slumber slips
Away like water, when I hear
The matchless music of her lips.

With her full beauty thus possest,
As flowers beneath the mid-day sun,
My drooping head upon my breast,
I swoon with sweetness till she's gone.

IF LOVE PROVE NOT UNKIND.

If Love prove not unkind
  Joy gushes forth in tears,
The fountain of my mind
  Flows down, and overbears,
As snow, dissolved in drops,
  Streams through the valley wide,
From the high mountain-tops
  On to the sea-green tide.

43

But when Love bloweth cold
  My mind is dark with doubt,
And Nature seemeth old,
  And the high hills about
Re-whiten with the blast,
  And streams, with frozen locks,
Grow mute and overcast
  Among the blue-cold rocks.

LOVE'S MEMORY.

THE cloud remembers the hill,
The moon remembers the sea,
The dew forgets not the rose,
And I will remember thee.

The blue tide foams on the shore,
With its passionate kisses wet;
The winds have their trysting-place,
Then how could my soul forget?

Soft as the rose-leaf falls,
By spirit-fingers prest,
So sweet thy memory lies
Full-perfumed in my breast.

ALL THINGS DELIGHT IN SLEEP.

ALL things delight in sleep,
  Morning to eve inclines,
Slowly the purple-woven shadows creep,
  And Heaven moves onward with its myriad signs
Above the watery deep.

At noon, among the hills,
  The shepherd makes complaint,
At even, to the murmur of soft bells,
  Leads his flocks downward to the valleys faint
With blowing daffodils.

A thousand minstrels throng
  Daily amid the wood,
At eve the burden of incessant song
  Fails to the minute note of solitude
The dropping shades among.

The bird is in the nest,
  The lamb is in the fold,
The day is crimson-cradled in the west,
  And all the argent heaven o'ershot with gold;
Only within my breast

Love, like a fury, wakes
  The secret, hidden fires,
That waste me till the rosy goddess breaks
  In virgin purity o'er Eastern spires
And silver-crested lakes.

LOVE NOT UNDERSTOOD.

LIGHT my love and airy is,
Forest-wild, with none to tame her;
And, because she knows not shame,
Nothing could shame her.

She so swift and sprightly is,
Toil or snare could not contain her;
And, because she stainless is,
Nothing could stain her.

Laughing, prattling here and there,
With a pretty, pleasing candour,
Could there any be would fail
To understand her?

Ah! they know not all her bliss;
She too pure is and too tender
For their Earth-philosophies
To mar, or mend her.

In its rich infinitude
Her sweet soul is to discover
By one only questioner —
Her own heart's lover.

I WOULD I WERE A PRIMROSE.

I WOULD I were a primrose,
Then, if my love came near me,
O would she not gather
And on her bosom wear me?

I would I were a lily
That blooms in the wood-places,
Then I know she would press me
To her lips, full of graces.

I would I were a sunbeam,
Then, till the evening closes,
I would lie on her warm cheek
With the milk and the roses.

I would I were the wild bird
That sings in the bushes,
For she would listen, listen,
'Mid the ferns and the rushes.

And if I were a pure thought,
As white as a blossom,
For ever would I nestle
In the sweet of her bosom.

IF LOVE CAME UNBIDDEN.

Widely I've sought you,
  Seeking and hiding,
Roses I've brought you,
  Joys undividing;
Roses for blisses,
  Ribands for binding,
Sweet are the kisses
  Follow the finding.

Often your laughter,
  Rippling through bushes,
Guided me after
  To the tall rushes;
Where you, low stooping,
  Looked oft behind you,
Fearing, yet hoping
  I should soon find you.

If Love, unhidden,
  Spoiled of the seeking,
Came forth unbidden,
  Ripe for the taking,
Who would not mourn him,
  Moved with his mildness,
Pass by, and scorn him,
  After his wildness?

LEAVE ME NOT EVER.

THE full tide turning, half its journey done,
  The evening poplar sighing o'er the river,
Showers of arrows from the setting sun;
          Leave me not ever.

Long purple shadows over hushing hills,
  The drowsy bee's late note, the night-wind's shiver,
The low-breathed litany of dying bells;
          Leave me not ever.

The twilight trembling over cooling springs,
  Heaven's archèd glory gone unto the Giver,
And darkness with obliterating wings;
          Leave me not ever.

Dew on the bending grasses, and a dream,
  Wavings of sleep above the stilly river,
And broken brightness of the pale moon-beam;
          Leave me not ever.

A cloud of anger was above my head,
  Love's truest triumph follows the forgiver,
The night is waning and the morn is red;
          Leave me not ever.

THE TRYST.

SHE came not as she said,
And my thought troubled me,
While the high sun, rose-red,
Sank down the western sea.

She came not when the skies
With faintest hues were flushed,
And, like the hushing noon,
My very soul was hushed.

She came not when the dusk
Had purpled all the hill,
And God moved in the heaven
His purpose to fulfil;

But, ere the blood-red star
Stood flaming on the height,
O! then my love returned,
And brought a swift delight.

Flower of my soul! the rose
Were no more dear to me.
Ah! that I could but share
Her sweet humility.

HASTE HITHER,

Haste hither! Love waits but an hour;
  Let not the god appeal in vain,
Nor idle hold his passion-power,
  Lest he not suffer it again.

To-day the lily blooms, then change
  Corrupts it, and the petals fall
They know not whither. Sweet and strange
  The moss-rose hangs on the garden wall,

Drinking the honey dew. Too soon,
  Dreaming still of the twilight dawn,
Unconscious in the noiseless noon,
  She flutters down to the grass-green lawn.

And Love, and Youth, and Happiness,
  And Hope, companion of our spring,
Will leave us prey to heaviness,
  Spoiled of our brief imagining.

THE WOODLAND.

I WANDERED in the woodland —
Young Niam loves it well —
Where the smooth-lipped, purple streamlet
Falls tinkling down the dell.

The woven branches scattered
A holy shade around;
The flowers of Earth, in beauty,
Were springing on the ground

Roused by the sun's warm glances,
In sweetest mystery —
The fern, and rose, and blue-bell,
And faint anemone.

I kissed each pure, pale petal,
And strained them to my breast;
The joyous thrush sat trilling
To his mate upon the nest.

Proud of the spoils I gathered —
My thought was very sweet —
I turned, and, in the road-way,
Young Niam soon did meet.

O happy heart of lovers!
My gems I straight let fall,
For she's a lovelier blossom,
The sweetest rose of all.

BROKEN VOWS.

You sware that you would love me
  Here, underneath the rose,
The blue heavens high above me,
  Day drooping to its close: —
"While purple Life complieth
  With woven will of Fate,
As this dim shadow lieth
  Intranced upon the gate."

The sun-set, yellow streaming,
  Burned on your slumbrous hair
Like golden arrows gleaming
  On seas of gossamer;
I caught your whisper dying
  From crimson-rosy lips,
Like faint-souled breezes sighing
  O'er summer-calming ships.

Ah! broken is the binding,
  Your vows are nothing worth,
Your silken cords, unwinding,
  Fall on the chilly earth;
Your honey-baited wooing,
  Love tokens, cruel-kind,
Have wrought a soul's undoing,
  Nor left a hope behind.

TIME HEALS ALL WOUNDS BUT ONE.

Time heals all wounds but one,
  That, hidden in the breast,
Burns like a furnace, or still smoulders on,
  And will not let the weary sufferer rest;
Time heals all wounds but one.

Time heals all wounds but one.
  The mother mourns her child,
The warrior weeps above his stricken son,
  Soon all their heavy sorrow is beguiled;
Time heals all wounds but one.

Time heals all wounds but one.
  The summer blossoms pass,
The gay companion of the rose is gone,
  New glories glow upon the autumn grass;
Time heals all wounds but one.

And ah! that it would heal
  The woe that is my own,
And from my wounded bosom softly steal
  The broken arrow-points sunk midway down;
Ah! Time, that it would heal!

Time heals all wounds but one,
  And will not brave the worst;
Hearts that are broken brokenly live on,
  And darken till the prison-fetter burst;
Time heals all wounds but one.

LEAVE THY HAUNT.

LEAVE thy haunt, deluded lover!
  Hidden field, and hoary wood,
Thou wilt never, never move her,
  Crying to a solitude;
She will more and more disdain thee,
  Name thee less and less in might,
Deeply wound and hourly pain thee,
  If thou failest in the fight.

Love owns not the craven-hearted,
  Such as cast away their shield,
Soonest met and soonest parted,
  Flying from the battlefield;
But who fighteth and remaineth,
  Scaling high the dizzy wall,
Every blushing honour gaineth
  When the towered city fall.

Wherefore, leave thy haunt, pale lover!
  Deck thee forth with helm and crest,
Many are the means to move her,
  Solitude availeth least;
Wave thy banner proudly o'er her,
  Claim her as thy lawful prize,
Prostrate all thy foes before her,
  And upon their ruin rise.

ALL NIGHT I LAY IN LOW DESPAIR.

ALL night I lay in low despair,
  Torn by a tempest, passion-deep,
And, while my lips were framed to prayer,
  My blinding eyes would weep.

"Great Love," I cried, "if thou hast ears
  And art not wholly reason-blind,
If pity may be taught with tears,
  Look in my steadfast mind!

"Behold! the little all I have
  I give thee; freely take, and twine
Thy tendrils in my heart, and save
  This watcher at thy shrine!

"My soul is dark with treason-blots,
  That I have surely sinned, I own,
All day I wander in deep grots
  As speechless as a stone;

"Or where the mill-dam sleeping lies,
  A pure, unruffled, scented pool,
Or welter under cloudless skies,
  Untaught in Wisdom's school!

"But though I move abroad unseen,
  In leafless groves, and balmless bowers,
Yet I have kept thy memory green
  And decked thy shrine with flowers!

"And I have plucked a trembling rose,
  And laid it on thy altar stone,
With incense of a hundred vows,
  Each tendered with a moan!

"Yet if I suffer what is just,
  And justice prove aright in thee,
Then I will suffer for I must;
  Pour all thy wrongs on me!"

Love heard, and from his shining height
  Smiled on my sorrow, gentle-wise;
Peace fell, and rivers of delight
  Fast flooded in my eyes.

LOVE'S VICTORY.

THINK you, with studied cruelty,
  And armour of a stormy face,ʻ
And wrath, and incivility,
  And graceless poverty of grace,
That you will shake the brazen tower
  Of my strong will, and banish thence,
With woman-anger, passion-power?
  Love taken in a weak defence!

But I have heard your humbleness,
  And know you won, ere strife begin;
Small strength, to arm your feebleness
  With hope of conquest, weak within!
I know, by that same heraldry,
  And his soul-shaking battle-cry,
That Love has gained the victory,
  And·ended your supremacy.

DEAR LOVE, FORGIVE.

DEAR love, forgive,
  In mercy hear me,
Let me but live
  A little near thee;
Here, lowly stoop,
  And own my sinning,
And dimly hope
  A new beginning.

O love, the wrong
  My anger wrought thee,
Stilled all my song.
  I have not sought thee
With heart uplift
  And proudly swelling,
For some rich gift
  From thy high dwelling.

Here as I come
  Low, humble-pleading,
My heart is dumb
  And dead with bleeding;
Pale, withered forms
  Fly on before me,
A hundred storms
  Have broken o'er me.

Dear love, forgive,
  In pity hear me;
Ah! let me live
  For ever near thee;

Full sad and strange
  Were all about me,
If I should range
  This world without thee.

NOBLE HEARTS.

To seek for grace where grace is not,
  To look for love with loveless eye,
To lighten Passion's foulest blot,
  To conquer hate with jealousy,
All this blind, poisoned hearts will prove
When senseless stones rise up and love.

Impassioned souls are highly strung;
  Thin reeds small winds will move apart;
One drop of anger, darkly wrung,
  Will leaven in a noble heart;
Unworthy fires droop one by one,
As stars are banished by the sun.

Love, full of generous disdain
  For wasting spites, and trifling jars,
Will stoop and sweep into the plain
  Provoked to equal-minded wars;
Will shoot his arrows wide around,
Give blow for blow, and wound for wound.

A KISS.

I AM happy to-night,
  The reason is this,
She stooped from her height,
  And yielded a kiss;
Above her the skies
  Their mysteries spread,
And full were her eyes,
  And drooping her head.

O pleasure deep-drawn,
  The crowning of bliss,
The joy of a dawn,
  The sweet of a kiss!
The thrill of delight,
  The throb of the brain,
And vision too bright
  To grasp it again!

The gloss of her hair,
  The glow of her cheek,
What flower could share?
  What poem could speak?
Soft lustre of eye,
  Still heaving of breast,
A beam from the sky!
  A breath from the west!

I am happy to-night,
  The reason is this,
She stooped from her height
  And yielded a kiss;
That rich treasure-trove,
  Nor glories of ships,
Shall ever remove
  Or snatch from my lips.

60

THE DEFENCE OF LOVE.

Hold me not guilty. Love was not to blame,
I have not sought thee with untrue desire,
To thy heart's love my heart could not aspire,
Nor have I known the crimson blush of shame;
But O! a fever wastes my lanquid frame,
My ears are dinned with sounds of silver wire,
The blood burns through my veins like liquid fire,
And I am all a-weary since you came.
'Tis not my fault, but my unhappiness;
Now never eve is sweet, nor morn is fair,
And Joy comes not, and Beauty moves apart.
Yet, if it must be so, will I no less,
In fullest purity, grant thee a share
Of the most secret passion of my heart.

THE RENUNCIATION.

When I do lie and watch the dawning break,
Flushing with gentlest hues the star-sown skies,
Reading Heaven's mysteries with long-weary eyes,
That peaceful honey-slumbers would not slake,
Or musing in the stillness half awake,
As a pale-featured flower dreaming lies,
Then oft my heart is pained to sweet surprise
With thought of what I suffer for love's sake:
But it is ended now. No more. For lo!
The early dawn-rose withers, the pale beam
Burns to a brightness, and the flame is fled.
The world grows dark about me. I will go,
Seeking within my soul a surer gleam,
Or follow where my spirit-love is sped.

61

NOT TIME, BUT LOVE.

Am I grown old? Ah no!
  It cannot, must not be,
If I am altered so
  'Tis Love hath wasted me.

Here with the glass! If age
  Have passed the middle prime,
And darkened half my page,
  It is not Love, but Time.

If many years have writ
  Their tale of added woe,
Love may be blameless yet,
  Then blameless let him go!

But if my sands of years
  Are not run midway out,
If no dark sign appears,
  Nor growing room for doubt,

Then lay the shame on Love,
  More cruel-fierce than Time,
And I will patient prove,
  And end my halting rhyme.

It is not Time. Ah no!
  My blood is leaping yet,
My tide is at the flow,
  My laurels surest-set;

Wherefore, I needs must own,
  If any changing be,
'Tis Love, and Love alone
  That hath so wasted me!

THE PASSING.

Ah! not to hear thy voice again,
No more to see thy face,
To wander unbeloved of men —
Earth were too drear a place!

Without thee, all were stark and cold,
Life but a graceless boon,
As joyless as the skies, that hold
The grey and withered moon.

No more I pleasure in the wood,
Or wonder at the skies,
But watch, in speechless solitude,
The death-cold mist arise;

And I must follow, while the Shape
Leads ever on and on,
To where the last dark shadows gape
Behind the setting sun.

THE ABSENT.

SEASONS may pass, Earth blossom red and gold,
Lily and rose with honey-dew be wet,
Or Nature's myriad mouths be stopt with cold,
   But love will not forget.

Ah! though in exile from thee I shall live,
Sundered by leagues of mountain and of sea,
Still to my throbbing soul shall Nature give
   Sure memories of thee.

Thee will I gather in the vernal wood,
Plucking thy sweetness with the violet dim,
And view thy beauty in the bursting bud
   Beside the river's brim;

Or, where the slender stream drops smoothly down
The sloping shadows with a dreamy tune,
Hear thy lip-music mingling with its own
   Beneath the rising moon.

Pure in thy thought as Love's own sanctity,
Rich as the rose before the sun is set,
The white dawn wakens; I must pass from thee;
   And thou? Wilt thou forget?

LEAVE ME ALONE!

LEAVE me alone!
  I will not fear,
Day is not flown
  Though night be near;
Burns still the stream,
  Glows yet the grove,
Here let me dream,
  Leave me, my love!

Leave me alone!
  My bark shall glide,
I will swim on
  Above the tide;
No wild sea-bloom
  Shall draw me down;
I know my doom,
  Leave me alone!

Leave me alone!
  Violet night
Fluttering down
  Falls on the sight;
Day passes by,
  Evening's soon gone,
Here let me lie,
  Leave me alone!

THE PROMISE.

SHE has promised, and I know
Love will not the debt forego;
Love would not the sin forgive
If she suffered doubts to live.

She has promised, and she gave
All the faith that lovers have;
Her full soul's intensity
Spake in earnest unto me.

She has yielded what I sought
In the furnace of my thought,
In the passionate unrest
And the tumult of my breast.

Therefore, leave we now to fret,
Since her love will not forget;
This the most my heart could crave,
This the promise that she gave.

JOY.

Now to my panting heart
Be Joy's true token;
No more to move apart —
Love has not the promise broken.

Vex not, and be not vext,
For hope's new risen;
Lo! soaring unperplext,
My soul has burst her prison.

Joy! Though we may not meet
In other union,
No power could spoil the sweet
Of our spirit's full communion.

Joy in the meadow still,
And the wood waking,
And in the deep heart-thrill,
With love's pure passion shaking.

III.

NATURE POEMS.

NATURAL THOUGHTS AND SURMISES.

I.

LONG time revolving within myself, and breathing heavily,
As one o'erfraught with anguish, stooping to moisten
My life's lips at the dried-up river of thought,
My very soul athirst, my brain and body melting,
And the sweet, fleshly compass of my heart consumed
With the inward, all-devouring, passionate interest
Of dateless sympathy, and slow-burning furnace of desire;
Now sitting at the foot of a gnarled and knotted oak,
Now hidden in delicious glooms of dark-tissued leaves,
Or bordering on the brim of a quiet, contemplative pool,
Or lying with my head pillowed on the cool mossy
    bank,
Or beneath the smooth-jointed, depending beeches,
Or stretched beneath the large oval-bodied elms,
Sometimes walking with my head and body bowed
In sorrow to the earth, with slow deliberate footsteps,
And now with head erect, every sinew strained and
    tightened,
Pacing with a lively exaltation, my arms and hands
    uplifted,
Drawing enraptured breaths, my heart and soul again
    dilating —
Or now again, closing the windows of my eyes, and
    listening intently
To the low ravishing enchantment of the winds con-
    ferring with the leaves,
Or the faint, far-off note of the ascending skylark,

Or, maybe, a melodious thrush warbling in the bush
    yonder,
Or gold-billed blackbird singing divinely to his mate —
Out of the deep and fathomless treasury of my soul,
As a little child gathers his lap-full of wild flowers
    by the waters,
So gathered I this posy of poor thought.

II.

Why do we two alone dreaming lie in the gloom of
    the hazel?
Or, bending over, seek our reflection in the quiet,
    complacent pool?
Or sleeping a moment, strong-clasped in the arms of
    the oak-tree there?
Or stretched like a shadow on the bosom of the sweet
    green turf?
Or playing like children with the diminutive water-
    brook?
Or listening to the murmuring insects and cheerful-
    humming bees?
Or the birds chanting their canticles in the wood
    yonder?
Now clasping in our arms the delirious wheat-sheaves,
Or staining the fabric of our lips with dewberries,
Or O, reverting to yon dim passionate slope
Crowned with the battle-scar of centuries there!
Yet ever winding back from the haunts of men, ever
    retiring
From the world's touch, ever fearing and trembling

As a tender, sensitive plant, cold-shaken with the
   tempest,
With the withering tempest of life, O my soul?

III.

O thou symbol, sign, and history, thou the question
   and the answer,
Thou the thinker and the thought, the puzzle, grave,
   complex, mystical,
The looser and solver of the same, the judge and
   judgment,
The divine factor of laws, briefs, rules, commentaries,
Yet holding nothing sacred but thyself, no law other
   than thyself,
Having no sensible beginning, fearing no sensible end,
Boundless in time, unfettered in thought, feeling not
   distance,
Flitting from world to world, from one universe to
   another,
Reading unwritten runes and letters of thoughts, dis-
   covering strange secrets,
All creeds and qualities, human and divine, causes,
   constituents;
Why this world's fast and fixed, like a jewel set firm
   in its socket,
And why the next one to it wheels and revolves, ever
   running round;
Why some stars assemble and meet together—or
   appear to do it—
As dear, kind-hearted friends, familiar, and trusting
   one another,

73

And why others glare with a terrible eye over measureless distances,

As burning to engage in a war of utter destruction and death,

Envying, like mortals, not only the unspeakable dust of a kingdom,

And that more than worthless rustle of pomp, and slow consuming pride,

But even the knowledge of an existence beyond themselves;

And now with an eye filled with pity, yet brimming with displeasure,

Regarding this infinitesimal something which philosophers call Earth,

Where one nation is at war with another, and every man with himself,

All honouring the same God, with here and there a difference,

Yet worshipfully kneeling at one shrine, and bowing to Advantage;

Some few loving without return—the sweet-smelling savours and odours;

Others hating without reason and remorse, never thinking why they do it,

Knowing neither the extent of their own shame, nor the misery they inflict on others;

One for an inch of territory waging incessant war with his neighbour,

Another furious if the light shine not first in his window;

This coveting a first in riches, and that in honour,

The soldier to be first in battle, the poet to be first at his trade,

The player and scholar first, the Cabinet Minister first,
Two discoverers arguing over the round pole of the world.
As if no mind but theirs could clearly encompass it;
The hare-brained inventor first, the sensitive musician first,
The smooth-tongued lawyer first, the certain politi-
cian first,
All aiming at pre-eminence, careless alike how they
come to it,
How many fall in the contest, foundations for their
pinnacles,
How many deaths and bodies they crowd beneath
their feet,
How many cries go up unheeded, and prayers unanswered,
So they arrive at last, destitute, and triumphant,
Staking their all for a bubble, the paltry possession,
That certain-speeding Death will surely deprive them of;
But though this is the goal for all, the pulse and
the passion,
The beginning and the end, and the common course
of things,
Thou wilt not mar that sweet sacred image of thyself,
Nor quit thy perfect, natural, safe tranquillity,
That art the true, eternal part of me, the date and
the inscription,
The living letter writ, now half-contained in the envelope
Of a poor, crumbling, diseased and decrepit body,
At this time half way to death, half old, and ripe for
dissolution.

IV.

Lo! who is the rich man, and who is the poor, and
what is a sufferer?

And what is all this I hear about tumult, strife, and division?

Are the rich desirous of things they have held, their states and possessions?

Is it natural for the king to cast away his crown and divest himself?

And do they that are worthless and poor covet to lose their poverty,

The sick man desire strength, the bones and sinews of another,

Or haply some poor relic of goods that falls from his table?

As the grass of the field, and the foliaged tree, it is natural.

For myself, I care not to be any other than I am,

For all the riches I have is nothing, and yet I am wealthy.

All that my more fortunate neighbour possesses I possess,

And often derive more pleasure from the thing than he himself;

Whatever the day brings forth, I am fully indifferent to it;

If the serial sun shines over the blue of the hills I am content;

And if the wind roars through the trees and the swelling raindrops with it, I am content.

I do not run into ecstasies over nothing, nor fashion ills for myself,

Being naturally mortal we shall learn the future soon enough.

V.

There you have the reason, in that you may fully
    understand it—
Putting the world aside, that cannot take measure of
    itself even,
Too dull to learn, too deadly gross to sympathise,
Treading Life's jewels in the slough beneath its feet —
Why this high pillar of an oak, broad elms, and hanging
    beeches.
This gentle-sloping hill, with the running stream
    beyond it,
This divine sweetness of flowers, and birds innumerable,
Green crowns of woods, pleasant and cool in summer;
This little silver pool, shallow and pure in the sunlight,
This gold-crimson of meadows and corn with the
    reapers in it,
This broad and ample valley, with the West Wind
    faintly audible,
And this beloved solitude, dear now as the mother of me,
Are fellowed with my soul in such affection:
It is because the same spirit that moves them moveth
    me also;
I am a part of them all, I owe nothing to heredity.
Flesh and blood are my dwelling, I am not the house itself;
Lo! I change my habitation, I put off mortality, but
    I am not another;
Whatever phases the earth runs through, I shall continue;
I have power over myself and over death, I do not
    intend perishing;
Yet when I choose to put off my body I shall very
    nearly deceive myself,

And strive, in temporal weakness, to baffle my own
loving purpose.
I shall see the several mourners arrive, the small
procession,
The women and children waiting round, the earth
open to receive me,
The banded priest, and the sexton with spade in
hand—the digger of corruption;
They will but deceive themselves who follow me there
to interment;
The elements will have received me, they will breathe
me in their nostrils;
I shall sigh in their streets at midnight, and blow in
their faces,
Water their fields with showers, stream with the sun
in their windows;
They will wear me on their bosoms, and gather me in
their orchards;
I shall be the bright star, just setting in the occident,
The green grass under their feet, and the budding acorns,
The softly-whispered vow and swelling note of the anthem.
I shall flow with the rivers and tides, and be conscious
of it, and of myself,·
Because I have loved not myself, and craved no earthly
possession,
But saw my feature in the glass and duly marvelled at it,
Praising the thing created, and the vast Originator.

THE HILLS.

I.

O GLIMMERING landscape of hills, slow-curving and
    winding,
For ever beginning, and ending, and losing, and finding,
Chiselled, and graven, and wrought to a virginal feature
With the mind, and the scope, and the pen of all-
    passionate Nature;
Beautiful-braided, unbrokenly simple and free,
With the inshore green and terminal blue of the sea;
Wave upon quivering wave, intense with the sun and
    the wind,
Full as the ocean before and vast as the valley
    behind;
Emblem of purity, strength, all-virtuous pride,
Keen with the breath of the shore, and strong with
    the salt of the tide;
Fair as the face of a maid, and doubly tender and dear
Than the wistful soul of a child, or a falling, ineffable
    tear;
O dear to my passionate soul! what labours remain
    to be done,
What fights to be fought, what deaths, ere our spirits
    re-mingle and run
As the pure, sweet, sorrowful wave, from the sheltering
    valley and lea,
Is clasped, embosomed, and twined in the rapturous
    arms of the sea;
How long shall the prisoner call, the suppliant wait
The consummate kindness of Death, the ultimate
    wisdom of Fate?

II.

O quiet, contemplative hills, you mystical sages,
Ripe with the wisdom of years, and the teaching of ages,
Marvel ye not that I pine for the thought ye are
thinking,
And thirst in my soul for the passionate draught ye
are drinking,
Poured from the bowl of the sun, that, the June-day
long, doth shine
Over your knitted brows, with the stealing wrath of
the vine?
How I sigh for the knowledge that's hid in the hold
of your heart,
While the year draws mightily round, and one after
another depart
The faded blossoms of Hope and broken threads of
Desire,
Yet living, re-raised and re-kindled with the sun's
unquenchable fire?
Can I think that ye know not the secret of all that
appears,
Of the storms, and the floods, and the multitudinous years,
The climates, and seasons, and revolutions of change,
How ye pondered and thought in your souls, and
counted it strange,
And writ in your innermost books, and brooded early
and late
On the boundless wisdom of Time, and dark
inscrutable Fate?
Ye know, ye know. I have heard you, loud and clear
as a bell,

I have learned from the breath of your lips, and
learned it truly and well,
And a tear steals down from mine eye and waters a
space on the sod,
And I rise from the region of man, and soar to the
borders of God,
And the fetters fall from my limbs, and the star of
my soul shines free
With the clarified hope of the past, and the mightier
future to be;
And I know in my heart, for I learned of the wind
and the sun,
That the hills, and the woods, and the skies, and my
soul will be one.

III.

I have come, O you hills! with the tremulous heart
of a fawn,
Quivering with passionate fear, in the grey-winged
hours of the dawn,
Ere the high, adorable East has unveiled, and unfurled
Her broad blue ensign above the boundless tracts of
the world;
I have come at your call, and fear lent wings to my feet,
With a cry in my soul, and the drum of my heart
a-beat,
And the streaming blood of the sweat slid down from
my brow,
As I clambered and came from the slumbering valley
below;
I flew like a flame, or an arrow that's shot in the wind,

With the glimmer of Truth before, and the shadow of
  Falsehood behind;
And the walls of the silver mist stood ever beside me,
And the flickering fire of the stars would never abide me,
So I flew with a hurrying haste until I had found you,
And threw, with the frenzy of fear, my wild arms
  around you,
And married the throb of my ear to the beat of your
  breast,
And strained with the strength of the East, and the
  nerves of the West—
So I caught that ye called me to hear, my beloved.
  'Tis done!
Now Earth has confessed, and I know that the hills
  and my soul will be one.

IV.

Tell me, you wandering winds, and passionate breezes
  that blow
Fresh from the concave shores of the globéd ocean
  below,
From what far-off, reverend fount are these streams
  that arise
And flood, with unquenchable tears, to the gates of
  my eyes?
This deeper, inconsequent, reasonless knowledge that
  creeps
Out of the innermost gulf of my soul's unfathoming
  deeps?
Thoughts and half-thoughts, like dreams, too vastly
  fragile and fine

For Reason's harrowing yoke, or the swerving,
  wavering line
Of the fleshly feeling of words, that clothe but the
  forms that have been,
And pall at the inward sense of the more than the
  vast unseen;
Come they not volleying forth, apart from the logical
  plan,
Less than the wisdom of God, and more than the
  reason of man?
Beautiful dreams, that faint for a far realising,
Yet ever, for ever, arising, arising, arising;
Near to the star of a thought, or bodying form of a
  word,
Shy as the rosy lips of a maid, or startled beautiful
  bird,
Trembling with delicate promise of "Yes," in hope to
  be given,
Or beating with slender and aureate wings at the dome
  of the heaven;
Ever and soon to be faltered and heard, the word to
  be spoken,
And ever the magical vision beyond, the spell to
  be broken!
O could I mightily grasp the symbol of Knowledge
  that lies
In the hidden hold of my heart, and tame the thoughts
  that arise
To a sober, sane confession of truth within truth,
And draw the delirious breath of the fire of my youth,
I know, in that passionate hour, my flickering torch
  must fail

Below the glimmering hint of a light, and pass, through
the veil,
Back to the august Giver that gave, that life would
be done,
And reason and silence of thought and my soul
should be one.

V.

Flow, endless rivers of thoughts and imaginings, flow!
And blow, you ministering, murmuring breaths of the
breezes, blow!
Over the ultimate hills and marginal blue of the plain,
Bending the passionate, reasoning blooms, and the
stalks of the grain,
Sifting the innermost soul of the woods, and thoughts
of the leaves,
Looping and twining your manifold arms round the
gold of the sheaves,
Blow softly, faintly, strongly out of the sea,
And blow the healing breath of the hills in the valley
to me!
I know, somewhere in my heart, that a thousand
enemies wait
To rend my quivering soul, but I fear not invisible
Fate,
Rapt with the calm, cool, sensible breath that distils
The clarified, purified, sisterly soul of the hills,
And I look in the glass of my heart, and hourly abide you
In the long, low evergreen valley that stretches beside you
O never shall the flattering cheer of the crowd, the
chink of the gold,

The pride of station and wealth be glittering fetters
    to hold
The scathless soul of the seer from the beauty that fills
The far, sweet visage of space, and the heart of the
    hills;
But ever while journeying wheels revolve in the race
    to be run,
So shall my heart beat true to the woods, and the
    hills, and the sun.

ODE TO MORNING.

Welcome to Morning! Now the shadows break.
    Living is Nature. The first songs arise.
The Angel of the East is full awake,
    And stealthy Dawn looks forth into the skies;
        And o'er the murmuring rills,
        And deeply slumbering hills,
The Spirit of the Earth breathes rapturous energies.

Awake, my soul! Awake from utter sleep,
    Death's poor beginning, the encumbering dream;
Soar from the Stygian bed, the crowded deep,
    The brooding waters of the Plutonian stream;
        Shake off the body's care,
        And through the crystal air,
Leap up to catch the Sun's ascending beam.

Look down into the east. How the day stirs!
  Tremblingly visible on the low-backed hills,
The light arises. Sable Night's wing whirrs
  Far to the west. A growing brightness fills
      The vast receiving space,
      And Morning's maiden face
Is tinged with roses and with daffodils.

Now vivider the light. The rose dies down
  Or melts, transfused into a clearer beam,
And the pure ore arises, like a crown
  On the World-Emperor's head, a glorious dream;
      And over-thwart the skies
      The gold-winged Angel flies,
Fluttering his mantle over vale and stream.

And lo! out of the bosom of the earth,
  Where he lay fondly nestling, now up-springs
The soaring skylark, this his second birth.
  How feelingly he talks! How loud he sings!
      Heaven seems to know the sound,
      And sheds a lustre round,
And rapturous Joy leaps down on his ethereal wings.

And thou, Fitzwarren! lying close among
  Thy wooded terraces of beech and firs,
Thou, too, shalt be remembered in my song.
  How peaceful are thy days! What passion stirs
      The heart within thy breast?
      Thy smoothly-slumbering rest
Has scarce been broken in a thousand years,

Save when autumnal tempests, howling bare
  Through thy warped foliage, scatter wide around
The everlasting leaves, and volleying air
  Rocks the tall belfry rooted in the ground;
      Or when an old elm falls
      Beneath thy antique walls,
And the low woods re-echo with the sound.

This is the home of Peace. Here Quiet loves
  To dwell with Beauty undisturbed, to be
At rest for ever. Blessed be thy groves,
  Thy wooded walks, thy old rusticity.
      Long may I find a place,
      Far from the reeling race,
To hold sweet converse with the heart of thee.

Now wonderful the meadows, calm, and still,
  And meditative yet, wrapt in the hues
Of Morning's rarest fancy, pure, until
  The vivifying beams new wealth infuse
      Of intellectual light,
      O'er-dimming Fancy's sight,
And heavenly heat sucks up the quivering dews.

But stay, impetuous one! Whither so fast?
  Here ponder by the stream that rolls along
Its full voluptuous torrent. Let us cast
  A thought to wood-ward, loitering here among
      Earth's faintliest uttered balms,
      And consecrated calms
Now fitly shattered with the bolts of song.

O secret wood! I know thy treasury,
   Thy full, embracing trees, the breath that flows
Through thy dim cloisters, weaving mystery,
   The open spaces, whither Flora strows
         Her intermingled sweets,
         Thy shelters and retreats,
The friendly company of thy leaves and boughs;

Yet, at this living hour, more dear thou seem'st
   To my affected fancy, and I feel
More animate with thee. Thither, as thou dream'st
   In thy compacted slumbers, would I steal
         Out of myself to be
         Lost in the soul of thee,
More beauty to confess or greater to conceal.

WINTER.

O Winter! loving and majestical,
Breathless, compassionate, mysterious,
Nature's reflection, the old earth's idleness,
Mother of glooms and shadows, free, tempestuous,
Raging and fearful, now brooding and solitary,
Now is thy time and season, thy throne and government.
The wind howls in the forest, the cloud hangs over
   the valley;
The sun creeps along the hill early to rest;
The round moon comes up over the dale, the stars
   glimmer and set;
The brown earth ponders, the woods mourn musically;

The yearlings crowd in the stall, the bared oak
quivers;
The chattering rooks dig among the leaves for acorns.
The thrush is mute in the bush, the blackbird sits still
on the bank;
The redbreast pipes cheerily, the pheasant hold his
perch in the tree;
Now the ice is over the pool, the frost glitters on the
window;
Suddenly the night comes down, the evening bell
arises;
The fire crackles on the hearth, the log emits an odour;
The children's faces beam with delight, watching the
flames go up;
The good-wife sets the table, hailing her spouse from
labour,
The crisp brown loaf, golden butter from the dairy,
The hot and steaming cup, cheerful and delicious,
And the strong dish of welcome, sure domestic comfort!
These are thy offerings, thy dear compensations,
In which my universal mind delights,
As one in reason and temperament.
Long may I walk the fields and terraces
Fresh with the crisping frost salubrious,
While the wind beats, in secret contemplation;
Wearing a heart as strong against misfortune
As the clear, cutting breath that smites my forehead.

THE EARTH LOVER.

To RICHARD JEFFERIES.

ALONG the beaten woodland track,
  Once more he trod with thousand fears,
And oft he pondered, looking back,
  And counting o'er the vanished years.

For O, his frame was poor at length,
  His withered limbs were spent and weak,
Sickness had robbed him of his strength,
  Health's flowers were faded from his cheek.

So, as he wandered on alone,
  And slowly in the woody dell,
Where the dead leaves came fluttering down,
  From his pale lips these numbers fell:

"And must it be that all around
  Will fade and wither on my view,
The spreading flowers upon the ground,
  And Heaven's high, soaring arch of blue?

"These woods of iron heart and strength,
  The sun's warm beam that shoots and thrills,
The stream that winds its sinuous length
  For ever downward from the hills?

"I would have tarried till the spring,
  Once more to pluck the vernal flowers,
To hear the mellow ousel sing,
  And feel the sunny April showers;

"But it is fated I must go;
   The cold wind shivers, death is nigh;
The Voice has spoken and I know;
   My days are ended; all must die!

"Yet other worshippers will come
   To pace the woods with happy tread,
While these poor lips are cold and dumb,
   And I am lying with the dead."

So said he, thus, and passed away
   For ever, and the winter flew;
The soft spring kindled day by day,
   Earth never more his footstep knew.

And all things quickened, one by one,
   The woods rang sweetly as before,
Joy scattered from the kindly sun,
   He only came not, evermore.

IN MY GARDEN.

To-day, within my garden arch,
   From the woodbine clustering round,
A dainty little wren down flew,
   And tripped along the ground.

Nearer the pretty stranger came,
   With pert and saucy pride,
Then nimbly hopped upon the seat,
   And waited by my side.

91

Quiet I sat like one transfixed—
    The sight was strange and new—
And wondered in my inmost heart
    What next the wren would do.

Awhile it stood, so pert and trim—
    My breath came soft and slow—
Now held its little head aside,
    And bobbed it to and fro;

Then, in a second, up it flew,
    Its little wings outspread,
Beneath the woodbine in the roof
    And perched upon my head.

I could have cried aloud with joy
    To feel its tiny weight,
But like a statue I remained,
    And still upon the seat.

Then off the little stranger went,
    And straight away it flew,
And out towards the elm-tree tops,
    Like a speck against the blue.

And now I know, what long I felt,
    With pain so sweet and wild,
That Nature holds me in her thought,
    And claims me for her child.

AFTER THE RAIN.

AFTER the rain,
New joy and beauty bringing,
  How sweet! to wander forth again
Where the loud thrush, singing, singing,
  Pours forth his soul and soothes the weary brain
With one full-hearted, loud, melodious strain,
          After the rain!

After the rain,
In the still evening, when the shadows thicken,
  And silence falls again,
Where the warm winds quicken, quicken,
  With their sweet and odorous breath,
  Every bud, and leaf and blossom,
  Drooping on the earth beneath,
While the soul to joy is fain,
Conquering every care and pain,
Let us wander forth again,
          After the rain!

After the rain,
The hills show brighter, their green slopes,
  Washed with the essence, purer, clearer,
  Are lovelier, sweeter, plainer, nearer;
Life stirs within us, and our hopes
  Kindling in the heart and brain.
Forthwith a rosier colouring assume,
Earth is studded o'er with bloom,
  Young we grow, we know not how,

Banished every toil and pain,
  As we see the red sun dipping,
O'er the meadows, tripping, tripping,
    After the rain.

THE FOREST OAK

WHAT'S Arthur, Lancelot,
Hecuba, or Helen,
To my forest oak?
Who sings of woody Ida,
Lofty Ida?
Of Ida, dewy-dark,
Ida, many-fountained,
Praising her piney timbers
Above my forest oak?

Did not dread Paris,
Seeking fair Lacaena,
Sail in ship of Ida,
.Drawing deaths and sorrows
On his parent city?
When the axe on Ida,
Wielded by the shepherd,
Shivered in the sunlight,
And the sounding echoes,
Rolling down the gorges,
Woke the timid maidens
From their noonday slumbers,
Was there any blessing
On that wood of Ida?

Why then sing of Ida
O'er my forest oak,
With his iron branches,
With his strength of ages,
With his towered greatness,
Standing like a giant
Grim into the battle,
High above his comrades;
With his trunk, moss-covered,
Old and weather-beaten,
Scars of many winters
On his wrinkled forehead;
Old and weather-beaten,
Young, and in his triumph,
All around his acorns
Growing into saplings,
Strength of mighty parent?

At his iron timbers
Many seas have shuddered,
Many hearts have broken.
When the booming cannon,
Hurling horrid thunders,
Battered on his bulwarks,
And the shots and splinters
Shrieked and fell around him,
Firm against the battle,
Forward in the firing,
Blackened with the burning,
Heedless of all dangers
Sailed my forest oak.

All the earth has known him,
Earth, and every ocean,
Winds and western breezes
Fly and fall before him.
Fled him, too, the Spaniard,
Frightened with his firmness;
Saw, and wondered at him,
Egypt and Egyptian.

Honour be to Ida
For her piney timbers,
And the waving ilex
Of the far Etruscan!
But not woody Ida,
Nor the far Etruscan,
Nor the towered summits
Of the Alps or Indies
Yield so rich a burden,
Strong, and lion-hearted,
As the stately pillar
Of my forest oak.

A WINTER'S EVENING.

Loud shrieks the tempest through the tossing trees,
  Wild, breathless winter shatters at the door,
The sad rose moans amid the trellises,
  The flying clouds a heavy deluge pour.

Along the hills, roused from their dreamless sleep,
  Faint in the gathering twilight, grey and bare,
The black fantastic shadows range and sweep,
  Or stream like banners in the moving air.

Soon, through the rift, the shining moon appears,
  A dim reflection in a watery glass,
Seen but a moment through the dropping tears,
  Then doubly thick the murky shadows pass.

So all night long upon the quaking roof,
  And in the chimney-top the tempest howls,
Rattling along the tiles with thunderous hoof,
  Loud with the fury of ten thousand souls;

Till rosy morning breaks with gentle light,
  Soft as a babe upon the mother's breast;
Below, the fields are gleaming silver-white,
  But the loud wind has roared itself to rest.

THE DAWNING.

WITH summer warmth the sunshine streams
  O'er hill and valley, heavenly bright;
Afar, the flooded river gleams,
  A blinding sea of silver light.

Dried are the dewy diamond drops
  That shivered on the acorn leaves,
And through the spaces of the copse
  Her thousand threads Arachne weaves.

Now chants the blackbird on the bush,
  Deceived with hope of early spring,
And on the tree a speckled thrush
  Opens his silvery throat to sing;

And stooping down, beneath my feet,
  Protected by the mouldering leaves,
And fostered by the kindly heat,
  The crimson-pointed primrose heaves

Her sturdy growth towards the light,
  In many a cluster richly set,
And trailing ivy, green and bright,
  Shelters the slumbering violet.

IV.

INDIAN POEMS.

INDIA: A POEM.

I.

Lo, where the sun, in his meridian,
With dazzling brilliance and imperial splendour
Smites with his burning rays the helpless earth,
Cowering beneath the fury of his eye,
With smouldering heat, intense and tropical!
Above the city, like a furnace blast
Laden invisible with particles
Of universal waste, that fret the eyes
And wound the parching cheek, the west wind sweeps
Withering each flower and herb. The buffalo,
From his hard toil released, with steady gait
To his loved mulberry-tree will soon repair,
And rest beneath the shade; or if perchance
Some lake or river, swamp, or reedy pool
Be near at hand, will there disport himself,
Swimming within the limits of the flood.
Not so the patient ox. He, yoked and bound
To creaking cart, or cultivating plough,
Toils hard apace, or on the threshing-floor,
In weary circuit driven, from morn till eve,
Tramples the ruddy corn. he may not eat,
In life-long bondage to the husbandman,
While children gather round and praise the scene.
Yet not the dusky native willingly
Braves the bright tyrant, though, but sparsely clad,
Half-naked, and with shaven skull exposed,

The Indian poems were written at Ranikhet, in the Himalayas, during the summer of 1918, while the author was recovering from fever contracted at Cawnpore.

Grasping his staff within his hand, he goes
Journeying to shrine or temple of the god,
But somewhere in the shade will rest at ease,
'Mid sheltering palms, or spreading mango grove,
Prone on the earth, and slumber through the noon.

Now 'tis the summer season. Midmost May
Burns at the height; the winter corn is cut;
The mango fruits are swelling on the tree;
Plantains are ripe; the golden pineapple
Sweetens apace; the jack-fruit's sickly odour
Wafts on the atmosphere of the bazaar,
And peach and apricot are new-arriving
Pluckt from the orchard bough. The noisy cuckoo
His shrill *Brain-Fever* oft reiterates,
Perched on the cotton-branch, and mocks aloud
The weary traveller who rest would take
In bower or arbour with clematis twined,
Or cool verandah 'neath the jutting eaves,
Where *pipal* and laburnum interjoin
Their branches, that with fruits promiscuous,
This with its treasury of golden blooms.
Nor doth the day, from morn till welcome eve,
Suffice him for his song, but still unweary,
When Night, with starry wonders manifold,
Creeps o'er the sky, he frets the listening air
Where bat, and flying fox, and owlet drift,
Uttering his loud cry shrilly 'neath the moon.
Nor he alone hath courage of the heat,
Though herb and tender flower be withered quite—
Save where, with leathern bottle at his back,
The naked *bhisti* coolly irrigates

The sheltered garden, drawing from the well
The precious moisture in his earthen bowl,
And imitates a deluge: now the *koel*
Utters his flutey note; the coppersmith
His mellow anvil beats; the tailor-bird
Cries frequent, and the gentle *hoopoe* calls,
And the hoarse crow, on tree or chimney-top,
Blabs loudly in his raucous monotone.

Now you shall see, where mighty Ganges rolled
Its sacred torrent through the fertile plains,
Bearing within its banks the melting snows
Of far Himālaya, Heaven's eternal seat,
A meagre, shrunken pool, not half its strength,
Flow listless through hot depths of drifting sand,
With not a sail, or oar, or skiff, or bark
Upon its idle waters to relieve
The desolation, but the shoals are strewn
With reeking carcase, skulls, and skeletons
Of beings long immersed by Hindu rite
And priestly ordinance. Above them stand
The greedy vultures, loathsome in aspect,
Or kite, or crow, that fatten on the feast,
With cries discordant filling all the air,
While silent floats the scaly crocodile
And scans his province for a living prey.
Yet even here hath cunning man contrived
To wrest a profit and his wants supply,
Sowing his seeds within the earthy bed
Of cucumbers and mallows, that will yield
Him recompense ere cometh the monsoon
And wash his labours downward to the sea.

But most the jaded city feels the heat
Insufferable, in street or alley packed,
Or stifling tenement, or dense bazaar,
Reeking with noxious odours, while within
His filthy den and sty contagious,
Where foul disease and sickness propagate—
Choleras, and fevers, and consumptions dire—
Crouches the native, his dear *hooka* nursing,
Expectorating freely in the sewer
That flows before his door, and still conducting
His meagre business. Unnumbered thousands
Throng in the narrow alleys, silently
This way or that deliberate proceeding
To mosque or temple, each his face besmeared
With sacred ashes, his true sect denoting,
Whether to Siva, Vishnu, or whate'er
Of god or demon he be consecrate.
Here, passed of all, spurned or unheeded, lies
A naked beggar, full of sores and wounds,
Expiring or expired, clothed not at all,
Round whom the teeming flies continual swarm
Offensive, loathsome with impurities.

Yet all the city is not fashioned thus,
For there are streets and ordered avenues,
Walks, parks, and fountains framed magnificent,
Roses and sweets where flits the busy bee,
Tall feathery palms, and spreading banyan trees,
Mosques, temples, pillars, shrines, and monuments,
And there a minster spire, with silvery bells
To call the worshipper, such as who heeds
Hears in a clime remote 'mongst other scenes,

Whose memory dear he prizes. Here to walk
At morn or eve, at sunrise, or at dusk,
In coolness of reiterated dawn,
Or glimmering twilight's dim intensity,
And wafted with soft airs and downy wings,
Were witching wonder, not to be compared
With aught Imagination might conceive.

Lo, where the loud drum beats, and solemn strains
Waft on the air, of flute-like instrument,
And the crowd thickens! 'Tis a funeral
Of native Hindu. Him the gods have called
Far from this pigmy plot of nether earth
To grant him due reward or punishment,
Renewal of the endless lease of life,
Superior or inferior, beast or brute,
Or bird, or wingéd insect, fish, or reptile,
Brahman, or *bunnia*, following his deserts,
For such was his belief. His poor corse hurried
On stretcher rudely borne, with gleaming shroud,
Through the full market-place, without the city,
Recks not of either, all indifferent
To what the gods decree of good or evil.

Now come they where 'tis meet a pause were made
To consummate the rite, and on the ground
Place the unhallowed corpse. The instruments
Cease duly, and the drums no longer beat.
Forthwith, of logs prepared the pyre is built,
With leaves and grasses strewn. One folds the shroud;
This will the corpse anoint; that mutters freely
His incantations, powerful to prevent

Devil or demon, or what spirit soe'er
Hovers invisible. Betimes the corse
Upon the pile disposed, and all performed
Of prayers, or vows, with embers from the hearth
The fire is kindled, and the smoke ascends
Leaping aloft into the firmament,
And all the dusky followers, unconcerned,
Squat heedless, till the scorching skull be cracked
With blow well-timed to free the spirit forth—
For thus it is decreed— and vultures gather
Scenting on air aloft the feast unclean.

Now swift the scene is changed. The juggler next,
Well practised, subtle, smooth, and affable,
Fluent of speech, a master of deceit,
A wizard, or a Mephistopheles,
Compels the crowd to wonder, where he sits
In shady spot remote, and gathers round
The gaping multitude. He, vaunting much
His poverty of art, and still descanting
On matters practical, from his small bag,
Or wallet, that long age hath much abused,
Pours out his wonders inexhaustible
Of birds, and whistling fowls, and swimming ducks,
Jewels of little worth, rude toys, and trinkets,
Puppets and pigmies strutting o'er the stage;
With his quick breath a hundred forms creating,
Or seeming to create, where nothing was.
They, open-mouthed, stare hard and fast upon him,
Counting him next a god, and speechless stand,
Awed with his skill and science magical.

106

Or, peradventure, staggering 'neath his load
Of poisonous reptiles, smooth and venomous,
In bag or basket carried, or concealed
In the loose folds of his habiliments,
The poor snake-charmer comes, a dreamy youth,
With figure slender, soft, and delicate,
Ill-matched with trade so dire and dangerous.
He, loosing from their secret dark abode
His slimy serpents, and the hooded cobra
With gleaming eyes, erect, and sibilant,
Tames them to gentleness with notes low-breathed
From his weird instrument, and departs well-pleased
With the small offerings profusely made.

And it may be the ragged beggar brings
In pouch or wallet, craving audience,
Snakes harmless, without fangs, and mongoose fierce
For cruel sport and exhibition.
He, cold of heart, by nature pitiless,
And wanting in regard, the snake releases
And sets the mongoose on. Then straight ensues
A conflict, bloody, long, and furious,
Combatant with combatant to the death
Engaged, in slimy fold, with rage intense,
The curling serpent round his body twined,
Till through its head the crunching teeth have met,
And its dead body lies upon the ground
With but one wound, all limp and motionless.

Or, if these fail, that interest may not lack
And dulness supervene, there straight appears
The travelling mountebank, with bear well-trained

In cunning like his master, to provide
Rude entertainment, or with ape, more skilful
To pleasure with his mimic drolleries.
Hither will come the busy mendicants,
Grovelling abject, and *'Baba! Baba!'* cry
In crowds vociferous, for alms entreating.
Or, unabashed, his naked body sprinkled
With dust and ashes, and his shaggy locks
Matted and tangled, cometh the *fakir*,
Bearing his couch of nails, thereon to lie,
Suffering a voluntary martyrdom
For the high gods' propitiation,
Neglectful of the sun, that smokes and streams
From brazen skies vindictive, so he earn
Mute approbation, and such recompense
Of corn, or powdered *gram*, sweet-meat, or cake,
That will suffice him for his sustenance.

Yonder, where midway in the valley lies
The Ganges, sacred river of the plains,
And mother well beloved, who doth dispense
Her favours manifold, the husbandman
Toils ceaseless on his farm, his brown breast bared,
Naked his feet, and withered arms exposed,
With spade or mattock delving in the earth,
Or, with his faithful ox yoked to the plough,
The stubborn glebe up-turns, or from the well
With windlass fitted, draws the moisture up
To soften his brown lands and irrigate,
That in due season they may well receive
Or seed of *gram*, or cereal, wheat, or vetch,

108

Or bearded barley, ere the monsoon break
And all his fields enrich and fructify.
Nor doth his spouse refuse the exercise,
Though great with child, but labours at his side
Silent, and openeth not her lips, content,
For 'tis the law of *Karma*, and her fate,
And she eschews it not. Little they eat
From morn till dusky eve, nor much require,
To luxury unused, on homely fare
Subsisting, grains of rice, or *gram* for meat,
Juggery, or maize new-pluckt, and for their drink
Water, such as the nearest pool supplies.

Nor, were they with such appetites endowed
As craved luxurious fare, could they repast
Provide, so hard and meagre is their lot,
With penury opprest, since their full lives
Needs must be spent in servitude to him *
Who fattens on their toils, extortionate,
Extracting interest cent for cent, well-pleased
To fill his greedy maw with spoils ill-got,
And bleed his victims to the death, himself
Firm in the law, and still inviolate.
Yet in the winter season, when the sun
Beats not so fierce, and starry nights are long,
When oxen press the sugar-cane, and gleam
Nightly the fires to quell the raging beast
That on his timid goats would gorge and feed,
He with his friends may gather and partake
Of feast more sumptuous, of pork, or egg,

* The *bunnia* or banker.

109

Milk that his goat or buffalo provides,
Juice from the press, or wine home-made, with plantain
Pluckt from the tree, or date, or cocoanut,
Ere he to slumber will himself betake
In his rude hut of leaves or wattles made,
And the cool air his strength invigorates.
Little he kens of other circumstance,
Of states or cities far, or nigh at hand,
Since Knowledge ne'er hath turned her beams upon him
And he, by idle Superstition led,
Follows the course, and falls an easy prey
To sickness and to death, by fell disease,
Fevers infectious, or the cobra's bite,
And questions not the gods, nor aught conceives
Of faith misplaced, or high ingratitude.

II.

So many idle verses have I writ
In painful exposition of my theme,
Yet little is revealed, as who should say—
"And this is India!" But think not to hold,
By such imperfect estimate, that thou
India hast seen, who scans my page, for she,
The inexpressible, cannot consist
In shadowy imitations, but rejects
All other enterprise of hand and brain,
Since high Imagination feeble is,
And Art too impotent to speak her praise
Of tower and temple, marble palaces,
Shrines of the mighty kings, high citadels,
Broad spreading plains with waving palms above them

Mountains and rivers stretching to the sea,
Her gold and purple, pearls and ivory,
Her cinnamon, and spices, and perfumes,
Jewels and silks; but who would contemplate
The nameless wonders, rare, and manifold,
Must expeditionise ere he believe
One-half of the great glory that she is,
And all my efforts are of little worth.
Yet do I follow on as one enslaved,
Indifferent or to censure or applause,
Save that the Muses give, and no rest take
Till I have stood before the heavenly seat
Of high Himalaya, where my journey ends.

Now, while the summer is most tyrannous,
Scattering his fiery heat about the plains,
And half mankind are feverish and sick,
Ere the monsoon in wonted fury break
With raging seas tempestuous, go we hence
And seek the soothing climate of the hills,
'Mid scented pine and shady *deodar*,
Beneath Himalaya's snowy mountain-tops,
And live like gods at ease, in cool content;
Where fragrant rose and honey-suckle bloom,
And skies are tempered with soft draperies,
The streamlet aye goes tripping down the dell,
The merry cuckoo calls, and butterflies
Airily flit, the gentle showers descend,
Sweetening the air, and golden slumber falls
Light as the dew that sparkles on the grass,
And all things are at peace.

Two ways invite
The world-wide traveller; this, where Everest
Rears his eternal summit through the clouds,
And Kinchinjunga beckons on the air
By Sikkim, or where Nandadevi towers
In Garhwal by Kumaon, and looks down
O'er his broad empire of unchanging snows
And pine-clad vales beneath. Our way we take
Northward to Nandadevi, where the road
Climbs steeply through the hills from Kathgodam,
Past the blue lakes and groves of Naini Tal
Towards Almora, halting on the height
Precipitous, where deep the vale extends
Below the piney woods of Ranikhet.

Nor easy is the path, that upward slants
By rock, and crag, and cliff, and stony steep
Of yawning chasm or of black ravine,
By rushing torrent dangerously led,
Or on the fearful precipice's brink
Creeping like flies, now this way, and now that,
Ascending or descending mile on mile
Below the purple summits, that yet seem
More lofty, and to greater length removed
The higher we attain. But pleasant is it,
When the high sun looks outward to the west
And streams above the snowy mountain-tops,
To feel the cool wind wafting through the leaves
Laden with scents of flowers well-beloved—
Primrose and violet, lily, rose, and pink,
Jasmine, and hyacinth, and columbine,

And fragrant orchis, sitting there at ease
Musing amid the new-found paradise.

And there are sweets indeed, for never Nature
Fashioned a scene more fair. Far off the plain,
Viewed through the cleft above the torrent's bed,
Shows like the rolling ocean; opposite
The distant mountain shines; the forest grass
Gleams golden; green the oaks; the spreading chestnut
Droops with her burden of soft blooms; the pine
Stands stately on the summit of the crest;
While, rushing o'er the slopes, the rhododendron
Sets all the hill aflame with waves intense
Of deepest crimson, and the pomegranate
Breathes her bright passion, pure and exquisite.
The feathery palm is not, nor plantain oft
Appears, save where the hill-man high hath set
His habitation, perched upon the ledge;
But rose, and drooping fern, and starry gems
Of myosotis, and proud goldilocks,
Or tinted saxifrage, crown all the heights
With spring-like beauty and new loveliness.

Yet fearful is the eve when from the west
The golden sun descends, and night comes down
And the shade thickens. Then, from bristling cave,
And bushy den concealed within the cleft,
The savage brute comes forth, on slaughter bent,
Lion, or tiger fierce, or crouching panther,
Leopard or bear, lean wolf, or hungry jackal,
Whose noisy pack, by base hyena led,
Makes the night hideous. Or the elephant

With gleaming tusk, untamed, and riotous,
Seeking new pasture, tramples in the wood,
And wakes the echoes in the low ravine,
Where the shrill owlets cry continuous.
At such an hour the timid husbandman,
From his rude couch aroused, steals trembling forth
And his spent fire re-kindles, to avert
The danger from his flocks now imminent.

See where yon village lies below the steep,
By running streamlet and thick woods embraced
In glooms of rhododendron and of pine,
Rude, wild, and mountainous, Bhowali named!
How peaceful and secure the prospect seems,
And to thine eye ideal, that still would seek
Beauty, nor aught beside will contemplate!
Yet here are quaking fears and terrors wild,
Sudden alarms, blood-curdling shouts, and cries
Borne on the air at midnight, for the beast
Comes frequent, tiger fierce, man-eater called,
Cunning and old, and versed in ways of men,
Sure of his victim, neither doth he choose
Whom age hath wasted, or long toil reduced,
Sickness, or famine, or decrepitude,
But woman chiefly, young, and smooth of limb,
Maiden, or matron, creeping unawares
Through the dense thicket till he pounce upon her
And bear her shrieking to her doom. In vain
The careful watch is set, and hunters keen
Wait in the forest; the sly thief appears
And rends his prey immune. The dusky native,
Parent, or husband, now disconsolate,

Mourns feebly and is reconciled; 'tis Kali,
Goddess invincible, hath visited
Him with this sorrow, Lady of Death, who rides
Nightly upon her beast with flaming eyes.

So, after long descent, slow winding down
Into the torrent's bed, that's Kosi called,
Roaring like bull below the cataract
Where he goes plunging o'er the shattered rocks,
And climbing up again, where, overhead,
Huge boulders, slipping down, have stopped their weight,
And threatening frown upon the traveller,
Horrid, and vast, and huge, portending death,
Our journey we pursue.

                  Here, where the road
Is narrow on the ridge, mid-way between
The towering summit and the black abyss,
Pause we and wonder at the retrospect.
How steep and perilous the path he knew
Who, slipping o'er the brink precipitous,
Went headlong to his doom, dashed on the rocks
Lying invisible beneath. The sun
Streams gentle, and the air invigorates.
Aloft, on wing divine, the eagle soars;
The lizard is asleep upon the stone;
The sun-birds flash and glitter, while the dove
Croons on the bough her ancient melody,
And all the mountain-side is gay and glad.
Refreshed, our upward course we further take
By Kairna on the height, and follow on,

Resting at evening till to-morrow's sun
Shine on our right, nor longer pause, until
The valley opens wide, and on our eyes
The vision of Himālaya falls at last
Eternal, over shadowy Ranikhet,
That marks our journey's end.

                              Himālaya,
Thou snowy wonder, miracle complete,
The jewelled girdle of the Earth, sublime
With peak, and pyramid, and pinnacle,
Mid-way to Heaven in majesty up-rearing
Thy silvery summits, throned amid the blue
And airy deep, whose wide circumference
Stretches immense; where Time hath fixed his seat,
And the high gods have their dim dwelling-place,
Eternal 'mid thy starry silences,
And Night and Morning reign! whether at dawn,
When over mighty Everest the sun,
Rising august, shoots his translucent beams
O'er Nepal to the gates of far Kashmir,
And looks on Mecca and Jerusalem;
Or noon-day quiet, over all supreme,
Hath calmed the honey bee, and stilled the note
Of Nature's choristers; or Evening steal
Soft on the sky, with rosy features flushed,
And gold hair streaming, all her breast aflame,
Blooming intense; and, dropping from the field
O'er seas Arabian, and the sandy shores
Where Tigris and Euphrates meet, the sun
Slowly departs and lights the underworld—
Still thou art all my thought, and ever glorious,

Sweet, silent, wise, austere, magnificent,
Beckoning my spirit upward from the earth
To walk immortal on thy heights, to be
For ever with thee there in storm or calm,
Naked amid the elements, and unfearful
To share thy secrets, which the whispering stars
Nightly unfold, assembled on thy brow,
Or grasp Böötes by the hand, that steers
His toiling team through the wide universe.

Nor only art thou vast and wonderful,
For witching beauty and fair prospect famed,
Bearing thy weight of forest on thy back,
And snows soft glittering through the pure serene;
But thou art India's shield and her defence,
Rendering her kingdom all inviolate
With walls and fortress inaccessible;
And, hiding in thy womb the sacred founts
Of many rivers, waterest all her plains
What time thy melting snows, from dreams awakened,
Rush thunderous down the foaming cataracts,
'Mid gloomy cave and icy depth concealed
Of frowning glacier, till the stream forth issues
And shouts adown the vale.

                              Two roads appear,
This westward to the heights of Naini Tal,
That eastward to Almora leading. Here
The native village rests upon the height,
And looks towards the Pole. Below, the vale
Lies steeply, where the *khuds** go plunging down,

---
* *Khud* = hill-side (local).

Graced with the pine's green foliage. Circular
The space within, and all beyond the hills
Rise endless, pile on pile, till, lost to view,
They sink invisible, and, over all,
From sunrise unto sunset stands revealed
Himãlaya, prisoning the immortal skies,
From where high Nampa his proud summit rears
In Nepal, and hoar Nandadevi frowns,
And Trisul beckons unto Badrinath,
To skiey Kamet, and bold Bartakhanta
That looks abroad to Kashmir.

                              Nor is aught,
Around us or above, this way or that,
Less arduous, rugged, rude, and mountainous
Than the wild way we came; but, rocks and crags,
Dark chasms, cliffs, and jutting promontories,
Streamlets, cascades, and foaming cataracts
Abound, and, over all, the pine's soft shade,
Or oak, or rhododendron gleaming bright,
Chestnut, or walnut, rose, or *deodar.*
No fields or smiling pastures tempt abroad
The happy husbandman, save what he hews
With patient effort from the stubborn rock
That, crumbling inch by inch beneath his might,
Yields him at length this terrace for his tilth,
And thus he is content. For sunny pasture
His nimble flocks climb the steep mountain-side —
Ox, sheep, or goat, or dusky buffalo —
And graze promiscuous where the eagle soars,
With steady pinion beating up the air,
And greedy vulture watches for his prey.

About the woods the gentle antelope
Wanders at large, gazelle, and tusky boar,
Leopard, and fox, and bear, unkind to men,
Or skulking panther, seeking to destroy
Leveret, or tender kid, or whatsoe'er
Strays from the flock when sets the evening sun
O'er Jaunli, stooping to Afghanistan.

Yon road, that steep goes winding sinuous down,
Will bring the weary traveller at length,
By course circuitous, after long toils,
Unto Chaubattia; this way we take,
And mingle with the crowd in the bazaar,
Idling away the peaceful summer-time,
Sitting on stool, while he within discovers
His goodly stock of silks and merchandise,
His skins of leopard and his graven gods
Of brass and ivory, woollens from Kashmir,
His hides from Kabul and Mount Everest,
Praising them all with wily eloquence,
With native cunning seeking to deceive
The unwary victim, and his purse to empty
In payment for his wares o'er their true worth.

Or, if the time be fair, and we no less
Have leisure to dispense, there yet remains
To interest, if not to educate,
In divers toils and primitive pursuits—
The native smith, with forge diminutive
Of smoky charcoal, and loud ringing anvil,
Beating the plastic metal to his will—
Axe-head, or pointed spear, or hunting-knife;

The rude musician next, his strings adjusting
With art untaught to native violin;
This way the carpenter, with square and rule,
And tools self-made; or, with more artistry,
Carver in wood or ivory, intent
With zeal his flowery task to consummate,
And perfect his design; or dusky dame,
Sitting before the busy spinning-wheel
With nimble fingers her fine threads to lengthen;
Or weaver at the loom, with wool new-shorn,
And wifely wisdom, studiously engaged;
While sits her neighbour shrewdly in the sun
And turns the dusty mill, her corn to grind,
All silent, grave, and labouring at their ease
With skill self-conscious, plain and natural.

Nor is the market-place to be o'er-looked,
For much within may warrant our regard,
Of curious fruits un-named, save in the tongue
Of the rude hill-man, seasonable and ripe—
The golden *gobbas*, purple mulberries,
Mangoes and melons, ruddy cherry there,
Apple, and juicy pear, and apricot,
With gourds and pumpkins, rice, and sugar corn,
And all that Earth upon her bosom bears
Within Himālaya's cool and kindly clime.

But most in woods and groves is our delight,
And rocky streamlet in the narrow bed
Deep hidden in the hollow low ravine,
'Mid humming bees, and birds, and butterflies,

That flit from flower to flower with noiseless wing,
And spoil them of the sweets they would not give.
Or, sitting oft at eve below the *khud*,
Beneath the flowery rhododendron, there,
When all the west is golden, and the sun
Pauses upon the distant mountain-tops,
To watch the grey wolf creeping from the glen,
The panther tracking up the steep cliff-side,
To scent the jackal's breath and meet his eyes,
To see the leveret come leaping forth,
Or timid coney and grey porcupine
Steal noiseless on the grass, until the dusk,
Full of the pine's sweet breath, comes dropping down
And all obliterates. Yet there are beams
Potent to light the traveller on his way,
Of fairy glow-worm's lamp, or Will-o'-the-Wisp,
Shining in bank, or bower, or shady grot,
Till the round moon steals softly o'er the heights,
And all Himālaya is again revealed
In silvery splendour 'neath her ray serene.

Thus glide the hours away, from morn to eve,
Evening till dusk, and dusk to dawn—a dream
Of endless beauty wondrously conceived,
Wherein substantial things do occupy
The place where vagrant Fancy executes
Her flowery shapes and airy images,
With joy no less than she herself could give;
And though upon my ears are frequent borne
War's thundering dissonance, vibrating deep,
Rumours of mighty battles lost and won,
The fate of cities, empires, dynasties,

Monarchs deposed, assassinations,
Crimes bloody and unnatural, worlds in arms,
Unmoved I hear and further heed them not,
But muse beneath the solitary pine,
Contented with the fate that brought me hither
And in fair season hence will me dispatch;
Nor, slave-like, seeking to avert the end
That needs must come to all, for which I wait
Indifferent, hating nothing that is made,
But reverencing duly things most fair,
Justice, and truth, and love to fellow men,
In error fruitful, but secure in this,
That I am Beauty's lover and her slave.

EAST AND WEST.

I covet not the West with its soulless things,
The clash and flash of battle and the blood that clings
But I would have the East, where the lotus swings,
And butterflies go drifting with their sail-like wings.

I care not for the West with its clouded skies,
The cold and cheerless ocean, where the tempest flies,
But my heart is in the East, where the blue deep lies
Dimpled with the laughing waves that fall and rise.

I envy not the West with its thousand themes,
The grinding of the wheels, and the senseless schemes,
For gentle is the East, and my spirit seems
Walking in the wonder of a world of dreams.

I care not for the West with its wealth untold,
Where beauty is a prize that is bought and sold,
For the glory of the East when I would behold,
Is brighter than the rainbow hues, or sunset-gold.

Scentless is the West and poor in its device,
Frozen in its solitude of winter snow and ice,
But O! the East is rich with cinnamon and spice,
And the flowers are always blooming, like the rose of
   Paradise.

TO INDIA.

BRAZEN, and loud, and shrill, O land of the wide sun!
   calleth
Ever War's clamorous clarion clearly to thee.
Awake and arise! The blossom fadeth and falleth,
Withers the fruit unheeded, withers and drops from the tree.

Lo! from the battle-front thy chivalrous sons returning,
Bright with the spoils of war, victorious, and won their
   desires,
Proudlier now for the dangers shared, their intense hearts
   burning
Nobly with thought and with deed, and the patriot's
   passionate fires.

(Them I admire, in my heart praising their zeal and
   devotion,
But chiefest their cheerful mien, manhood, and splendid
   pride,
Scorning in treacherous act to engage, or by a commotion,
Basely to leave and desert the comrade that fought at
   their side).

But neither thy chivalrous sons, whom the great ships,
   homeward wending,
Speed through the purple fields to city, temple, and
   shrine,
Nor all thy noble victories past, and fame unending,
Serve to cover and shield thee safe from the foe's design;

Knowing that not once merely to have striven and won
   engageth
Haply perennial Peace, Earth's mistress, but ever to stand
Steadfast and true in thy soul to the shock of the storm
   that rageth
Near or afar, and threatens to fall like a curse on the land.

Wisely thy mother regardeth and loveth her children, tender,
Babe-like lisping her name, fed with the milk of her breast;
Yea! and will cherish and lead them, step by step, to
   the splendour
Of god-like wisdom and strength, the crown of the
   golden West.

RANIKHET.

Where Dawn puts forth her flame-white hand,
   And suns and moons successive rise,
Lo! Trisul, Nandadevi stand
   And prop the empire of the skies.

Westward the velvet glooms abide
   Till Dawn and Dusk have kissed and met,
And, stealing o'er the mountain-side,
   Part on the hills of Ranikhet.

124

Now south the circle runs; o'erhead
  The arching azure slow declines,
Whose gauzy veil is lightly spread
  Above her myriad oaks and pines,

Where burns the tiger, fiercely vext,
  The panther, crouching in his den,
And rugged lion, leaping next
  To rend the ruby hearts of men.

And there the snowy roof ascends
  Eternal, silvering in the sun,
And with the azure sweetly blends
  Till heaven and earth are mingled one.

TO THE HIMALAYAS

I MAY not walk above your heavenly heights,
Nor unto those ethereal realms attain
Where dwells Eternity, with all her train
Of suns, and moons, and stars, and satellites,
But since the universal Soul invites,
And Beauty beckons, from Earth's numbing pain
Invisible I soar, where, without stain,
Spirit with spirit, soul with soul unites;
Then thrills my essence with a joy divine,
Musing with Time and Silence, while the Fates
Croon their old prophecy of coming years;
For I am one with you, and ye are mine,
And my immortal spirit penetrates
Beyond the unimaginable spheres.

125

SWEET IS THE WOOD.

Sweet is the wood, and tender is the sky
Between the scented pines, that sing and sigh;
 The rose's fragrance there
 Is wafted through the air,
And on my cheek is perched a painted butterfly.

Above, the chestnut blooms, displaying wide
Her gaudy treasure, pink and golden-eyed,
 And where my foot is set
 The purple violet
Swoons with a pure delight upon the steep *khud*-side

Below the cliff sure-footed leopards dwell,
The cautious panther creeps along the dell,
 And on the flowery slope
 The slender antelope
Sports in the spreading shade with timid, soft gazelle.

Ah! life is sweetest here amid the trees,
And birds, and butterflies, and humming bees;
 But Nandadevi's snows
 Are blushing like the rose,
And crimson swims the sunset o'er the western seas.

NOON.

THE noon's begun.
See! where bold Trisul reared his hoary head
Majestic in the dawn, and, looking down,
Scattered the golden brightness of his crown,
A cloudy-woven canopy is spread;
The lion slumbers in the river-bed,
  And sultry is the sun.

  The pine and oak,
With tuft and tassel, from whose scented tops
The tangled winds have stol'n their sweet perfume,
Stand motionless. The rhododendron bloom
Burns with a flame intense and downward drops;
Tired with his toil, the jungle-woodman stops
  And pauses on the stroke.

  The sun declines.
Broke is the sceptre in the tyrant's hand,
The spell is ended, whereby he had made
A lifeless solitude in heat and shade.
Now stirs the lion from his couch of sand,
And the Himālayan summits cloudless stand
  Above the whispering pines.

AT RANIKHET.

I KNOW no sight or sound but seemeth sweet,
Green oaks, tall pines, and native drums that beat,
The children playing in the village street
Naked as God hath made them; even the thrill
Of distant thunder, loud upon the hill,
In me no fear or sorrow could beget
    At Ranikhet.

Bright as the rainbow-tint, above the snows
The Dawn steals down, and kindles as it goes;
The golden sun up-leaps; a soft wind blows
Wafting the pine-scents in an endless stream,
And life is peaceful as a summer dream,
That ends not, though the crimson sun be set
    O'er Ranikhet.

The day dies softly, morn to evening yearns;
Slow down the *khud* the patient ox returns;
The glow-worm's lamp is lit, the fire-fly burns
With scintillating brightness of a star;
Hushed are the noises of the loud bazaar,
Save where the Brahman's bell is tinkling yet
    In Ranikhet.

AFTERNOON.

    ONLY the butterflies
Are patient of the sun. The bee, that sips
The dewy souls of flowers, and homeward fleets,
Laden with golden joys and liquid sweets
(Where toils the hive, and fragrant honey drips)
Is fallen asleep within the lily's lips,
    Tired with his ecstasies.

Fainting, the rose
In sweetest agony her spirit yields,
Scattering her snowy image on the grass;
The rhododendron blooms, a burning mass,
Droop in the thicket of the chestnut shields;
Now come the weary oxen from the fields,
And the mystic buffaloes.

THE SNOWS.

BLUE is the vault of heaven, and deep
O'er Nandadevi's awful steep;
On Kamet's top the stars look down
And weave for him a golden crown.

On Nampa strikes the central fire,
And smites his soul to fierce desire,
By Bartakhanta pausing soon
To gild the sickle of the moon.

Between, in purple light and shade,
With dawn, and noon, and sunset made,
A solemn city there begets
With towers, and spires, and minarets.

My soul shrinks backward in amaze,
And half forbids the eyes to gaze,
Now, shooting forth, re-views the sight,
And leaps to haeven in sweet delight.

129

THE STORM.

THE clouds sweep down,
Ruffling the foliage of the pine-tree tops
With rugged pinions; thunder echoes soon.
Dark is the sky and sullen; now the noon,
That yielded to the bee her golden crops,
Is hid; the laughing rain descends in drops,
  And smokes upon the stone.

  The lightning gleams
Fierce through the heavens and livid to the Pole,
Nor heeds the Himalayan heights, that would oppose
Its path with threatening ice and freezing snows,
Like a red fury rushing to the goal;
Around, vociferous thunders rage and roll
  With inarticulate themes.

  I know no fear,
For why? My soul is peaceful as the dawn.
Let storms and winds their fitful course pursue!
The cloud will break, heaven blossom in the blue,
And the loud-pealing passion be withdrawn;
Pale Evening steals along the upland lawn,
  And golden lights appear.

MONSOON TIME.

Joy it is in Ranikhet
Walking when the eve is wet
Underneath the scented glooms
Of the over-arching pines,
Where the fire-fly flits and shines
In among the chestnut blooms,
And the glow-worm's lamp is set
To guide the feet to Ranikhet.

Ranikhet is sweet and wild,
Like a lonely forest-child,
Born in habitation rude,
Rocked upon the knees of Time,
Tutored to an art sublime
In her virgin solitude:
Happy is the day we met,
Mountain-maiden Ranikhet!

Ranikhet is soft and fair,
With the pine-scents in her hair,
On her breast a rose is worn,
With a ravishing perfume,
And a rhododendron bloom
Richer than the skies at morn:
So all my heart with love is set;
I'll live and die for Ranikhet.

MANA.

WHERE smites the sun on Mana's breast,
  And rock and crag tower in the height,
The eagle builds her dizzy nest,
  And leads her young in painful flight.

Far down, the thunderous torrents leap,
  Loud-echoing through the clov'n ravine.
Like music of the sounding deep,
  The spirits of the vast unseen;

(The founts of mighty rivers, soon
  To vaunt abroad their virgin birth,
And babble to the listening moon
  Their ceaseless wanderings through the earth.)

Dawn stoops above thy pallid brow,
  And binds it with a flowery wreath;
The crimson twilight swims below,
  And purple darkness hides beneath.

Upon thy height, in ancient time,
  The stars in solemn council sate
And nightly now the ether climb
  To muse awhile with Heaven and Fate.

IN KUMAON.

IN Kumaon the hills are bright,
  And mild the sun that shines there-o'er,
But sweeter is my heart's delight
  Than all the joys of Bangalore.

132

The purple mountain's solitude
  Has crept about my wondering soul,
And all my being is endued
  With Beauty's golden aureole.

I covet not the sunny South,
  With stately palms and shining seas,
The full meridian's burning drouth,
  Nor temples, tombs, and mysteries;

But tread the mountain-path alone,
  Where the blue heaven slow declines
O'er high Himālaya's silvery crown;
  Or muse amid the silent pines,

While sinks the sun into the West,
  And blushes on the northern snow,
And the white moon climbs o'er the crest
  High up above the bungalow.

EVENING.

PALE evening is over the blushing skies,
And the air is filled with faint butterflies,
And bird-like moths, with wondrous wings;
And ever the cricket cheerily sings,
And the pine's tall shade
Creeps down the glade,
And the high noon-brightness withers and dies.

133

The lonely lizard, that loves the oak,
And sleeps in its branches, heavy and sound,
Is seeking its stony nest on the ground;
Far off the mountain-cataracts smoke,
And the wolf's low howl,
And the panther's growl
Alrealy I hear in the woods around.

The moon in her dream-like bliss steals forth
And silvers the snows of the vacant north;
A myriad fire-flies flicker and shine,
And the glow-worm kindles her taper fine,
Twinkling in the glooms
Of ferns, and leaves, and blooms,
And the soul of the night is poured like wine.

THE FLOWERS OF RANIKHET.

WALKING down to Ranikhet,
Eve and Doris sweetly met,
Setting out their laps to fill
With flowers that blossom by the hill.

All through the gentle afternoon,
While the lilies doze and swoon,
They ran, and plucked the gaudy store,
Then ceased, to tell their treasures o'er.

Said Eve — "I count the rhododendron best;
Her flaming soul burns redder than the West".
"Nay", answered Doris, "for I do suppose
The best and sweetest is this blushing rose".

134

Said Eve — "A crimson strawberry I found
With fruits and branches trailing on the ground".
Replied young Doris — "In a shady spot
I plucked sweet primulas, and touch-me-not".

Quoth Eve — "A spotted fox-glove here behold,
And evening primroses with leaves of gold":
And Doris — "Richer treasure have I yet,
For I have found the sky-blue violet".

"Ox-eyes are mine, and shut-the-eye-at-noon,
That's goat's-beard called", said Eve, replying soon:
"And I", said Doris with the eyes of blue,
"Plucked crane's-bill, marigold, and mullein, too".

"This purple speedwell here, with flowers so fine",
Said Eve, "was dreaming underneath the pine":
"And I", said Doris, "plucked this golden star
Of saxifrage beneath the *deodar*".

"Sweet is the jasmine scent that blooms o'erhead,
And berberis is sweet", Eve sweetly said;
Answered young Doris — "Hither as I came
This rock-rose kindled to a burning flame".

Now Eve — "As I was walking in the cool
I saw this crow-foot drinking at a pool";
"This slender willow-herb, with lips of red,
Was waving on the *khud*", fair Doris said.

Smiled Eve — "The blue forget-me-not is here,
Bugloss, and calamint, and eyebright clear";
And Doris — "Where the path goes tripping down
This dandelion wore his golden crown".

Continued Eve — "Beneath the chestnut shade.
Cinquefoil and avens have their couches made":
"And see!" cried Doris, brightening as she spoke,
"All these I gathered underneath the oak".

Then emptied both their laps, with childish zest,
Eager to count the spoils they still possessed;
There gromwell, orchis, nipplewort were found,
And persicaria, bleeding like a wound.

Above, the swallow twittered as it flew,
Swimming and circling in the liquid blue;
The merry cuckoo, with a flute-like throat,
Made the hills echo with his April note.

Thus, as the sun went down behind the snows,
And over Nampa's height the pale moon rose,
Were fire-flies burn, and glow-worms' lamps are set,
Eve and fair Doris came to Ranikhet.

IN WINTER THE HILLS ARE WHITE.

In winter the hills are white, then it is my delight
To see the creaking wain bring home the sugar-cane.
Oxen draw the plough smoothly to and fro;
Mango-trees are green; everywhere is seen
Springing blade and shoot, bud, and leaf, and fruit.
When sunny April comes the wild bee hums,
Rifling in the glooms of the citron-blooms;
Dizzy insects pass, settling on the grass;

136

Daily the bright sun shines through the silent pines,
Where the torrent leaps down the rocky steeps,
And the rapids smoke underneath the oak.
Now in the bamboo shade the reaper down is laid
Idly through the noon, while the wheat is strewn;
Fiercely smites the sun, summer-time's begun.
Evening, soft and calm, rustles in the palm;
Breathes the shepherd's pipe, mango fruits are ripe,
Peach with rosy spot, plum, and apricot.
In the month of June cometh the Monsoon
Swiftly from the South, to quench the burning drouth,
Like a thing of fear, frowning everywhere,
The lightning in his eyes flashing through the skies.
Thunder, too, he brings, hidden in his wings,
While the tempest sings, and the welkin rings,
As the laughing rain shouts upon the plain.

INDIAN HERDSMAN'S SONG.

Come home! Come home! 'Tis twilight, and day's ending,
    Cease now, ye merry kids, your sport and play,
The mighty god is from his throne descending,
    And, on his path attending,
Night hangs her silvery lamp to guide us on our way.

Come home! Come home! Where have ye strayed?
    O whither?
    Dark is the wood and fearsome where you bide;
Late, late yestreve I saw the grey wolves thither
    Returning all together,
With foaming mouths agape, and nostrils gleaming wide.

Through the blue heaven's dim veil the stars are peeping;
    Ah me! to fear my idle heart is set;
Or wolf or panther, through the darkness creeping,
    Hath found you tired and sleeping,
And with your crimson blood his cruel jaws are wet.

O, if my fears prove true, and I should find ye
    Bleeding and mangled with a deadly wound,
My flute and mantle would I cast behind me,
    And with sad garlands bind me,
And wake the listening echoes with a mournful sound.

Sweet are our daily joys, and pleasant wholly;
    Bright are the pastures whither ye are led,
Beyond the city's care and melancholy.
    At eve returning slowly
Where the dim skies are flushed and kindled rosy-red.

AT CAWNPORE.

Days of unclouded bright, where, 'neath the sweltering sky,
Quivers the panting earth, and the white blooms fade
        and die,
And the gold bee idly flits, and the powdered butterfly.

In the hot river-bed below, with shrunken streams,
The holy Ganges winds and dwindles, till it seems
Lost in the flaming south afar, in a haze of dreams.

The city's heart beats slow; now languid is the sight
Of the crowds down-moving in the blinding light
Through the long bazaar, with garments gleaming white.

138

In many an avenue, and many a glade,
The young rose droops and pines beneath the mango shade
Where, through the afternoon, the buffalo is laid.

At eve the high sun sinks, and o'er the scorching plain
Scatters into the West his showers of golden rain,
And beast and man revive, and thought stirs in the brain.

Now over all the dusk her scented mantle flings,
And a cloud of sweetness from the earth up-springs,
And the night-bird cries, and bats wheel by on velvet wings.

TO THE MANGO.

OF Hella's fruits let others boast,
And praise the olive and the vine,
Or search from distant coast to coast
For joy that shall out-rival thine!
Vain the quest, for there is not
Peach, or sunny apricot,
Nor scented paupau, fig nor date,
With sweet so subtly delicate
As Nature hath allowed thee,
And wherewith she endowed thee,
So queenly is thy state,
High and predominate.

Thou art of the earth and sun,
The ancient gods have made thee
For dainty food to feed upon,
Such honours they have paid thee!

Gotten in a golden dream,
By the ocean's sacred stream,
Ripened in the noon-day fire.
Drooping with a long desire,
Craving still and thirsting,
Thy soul with sweetness bursting,
Till all thy slumbers slacken,
And from dreams thou awaken.

ON THE BODY OF A HINDU FLOATING DOWN THE GANGES.

O WHITHER, like a shattered bark that glideth
  Bereft of sail or oar,
Wend'st thou thy course? What god thy journey guideth
  Unto what unknown shore?

Dark are thy eyes with dusk of death, that dimmeth
  Life's bright ·and radiant star,
All heedless of the purple tide that swimmeth
  Around thee and afar.

Clasped are thy hands above thy breast, and folded
  Within the clinging shroud;
Upon thy lifeless lips the speech that's moulded
  Is uttered not aloud.

Withered the ornaments that sometime bound thee
  When thou wert garlanded,
Swimming and floating in the deep around thee,
  Yellow, and white, and red.

Yet thou had'st faith and highest hope, unheeding
    The cynic's idle plea,
In the vext volume of Life's story reading
    Thy soul's eternity.

Ah! on my eyes, too, when the dusk descendeth,
    Night's darkness will be sown,
And where the purple river slowly wendeth
    Shall I set out alone.

THE SACRED BULL OF SHIVA.

When I view thee on the plain,
Seeking whither Shiva went,
In the sunlight's golden rain,
Stately and magnificent,
In thine eye the sacred fire
Of unquenchable desire,
By the god's high temple pondering,
Or in desert places wandering,
Over fields of springing corn,
With thy brightly gleaming horn,
And thy head to heaven up-raising,
Mutely on the ether gazing,
Almost I concede to thee
The spirit of divinity.

Free and noble is thy race,
The high god bows before thee,
His temple is thy dwelling-place,

141

His worshippers adore thee;
And devoutly thou art led,
And with fresh flowers garlanded,
When the happy day shall fall
Of the holy festival.
And maidens who have bound thee
Sing and dance around thee,
Praising Shiva the Giver,
Who ruleth for ever;
Giveth, too, and taketh,
Maketh and unmaketh,
Pleaseth and annoyeth,
Getteth and destroyeth,
So mighty is the god
When he rides abroad.

IF DEATH SHOULD COME TO ME.

If Death should come te me
On wings of thunder, rushing trough the deep
    Or on my senses creep
With beautiful soft calm, as when a dream
Steals from the golden sunset, and doth seem
Life's lovely counterpart, now viewed in sleep,
    I care not where I be,
If Death should come to me.

If Death should come to me
In shape unholy, shuddering on the sight,
    Or with a soft delight,
I would not flee the terror of his face,

Fainting to share the sweet of his embrace,
That doth to greater bliss my soul invite;
  But happy would I be,
  If Death should come to me.

LEAVING RANIKHET.

SPRING will wake and smile again lightly o'er the valley,
Spring will deck the woods with flowers and stir the
    sleeping pine,
Gay shall the chestnut bloom in the hidden forest,
Clear through the azure the gentle sun will shine;
Birds build their nest amid the honey-suckle,
Gleam the snowy pyramid where Trisul lies,
Clouds come and rest there daily in the noon-tide,
But never shall I stand and watch the white moon rise.

Spring will bring the laughing wind, rustling in the branches,
The heavy rhododendron will be musing late,
Blue will the hyacinth blossom with the wild rose,
Merry shout the cuckoo to his echoing mate;
Red will the skies gleam, lurid with the sunset,
Soft fall the twilight where the torrents roar,
Lonely the grey wolf howl upon the hill-side,
But Time will bear me far away, and I shall come no more.

V.

VARIOUS POEMS.

ABOUT WILTSHIRE.

SIMPLE are thy woods and valleys; homely are thy downs
    and hills,
  But thy fields are fresh and fertile, and a music stirs
     the glade
Where the golden furze is blooming, and the honeysuckle
    fills
  The air with sweet more tender than the hawthorn
     scent has made;
Meadows here and blooming orchards, groves of poplar,
    walls of willow,
  Spreading oak, and elm, and chestnut, arms and branches
     interlaced,
With the honey bean and clover, and the coltsfoot sweet
    and yellow,
  Like the letters on a girdle twined about a maiden's
     waist;
There the gods have ruled before us, worshipped once,
    and venerated,
  Tombs of endless storms and winters, simple, rugged,
     and sublime.
Monuments of kings and heroes, undeciphered and undated,
  Sacramental shrines and temples wasted with the wrath
    of Time;
Where the hills are strown with relics of old warriors
    and sages,
  Carved with strange and runic features, cleft with fur-
    rows long and deep,
Great with human recollection of the dark and troubled ages,
  And the battles of the fathers who amid their ruins sleep.

Land of health and flowing breezes, land of sunshine and
   of mirth,
Of the high and celebrated, of the humble and the free,
Happy in thy generations, dearest spot of all the earth,
   Mother of unnumbered children, hope and comforter to me!
Could I tell the love within me, could I show the pains
   I feel,
   How I hold thee in affection, how my arms would clasp
      and twine,
How I long to grow unto thee, while my heart and soul
   would steal
   Like a flame out of my bosom to that greater soul of
      thine?
All the passion of existence, all my riches and my wealth,
   All my earthly joy abounding, all of beauty or of sound,
All I hope for in the future, robust good and present health,
   All my being is concentered in this little plot of ground,
Here I live as one translated, careless in the world of toil,
   Pleased to wear the human fetter, journeying out along
      the road
With eternity around me, happy in my mortal soil,
   Climbing through the silent valley up the universe to God.

Blessing on thy fields for ever! Blessing and the crown
   of peace!
Joy possess thy straying hamlets and prosperity thy towns!
May the golden-gleaming banner of the harvest never cease
   To wave along thy valleys and to beautify thy downs!
May thy hills be rich with verdure, and thy meadows full
   and deep,
   Thy woods be rare with violet, to every eye endeared,

148

And let no civil strife arise, and bid Contention sleep,
  And O may Labour rest content, and Justice be revered!
To all thy yeomen, lusty hearts, fair tilth, and fruitful years,
  The simple recompense of faith, the sacrifice of pride,
A courage to thy ministers and wisdom to thy peers,
  And over all a lasting love, a friendship to abide!
Blessing on thy sons and daughters who have crossed
    beyond the sea,
  May fortune further their desires and plenty fill their
    store,
But O may kindness turn their thoughts in thankfulness
    to thee,
  To have thee in their memory still and love thee more
    and more.

MUSIC IN SALISBURY CATHEDRAL.

Footfalls, far, faint, distant, inaudible;
Saints' feet in the cloisters, a very hint of sound,
Increasing, yet subdued; like the wind murmuring
O'er deeply slumbering woods, ruffling the leaves
To lyrical protest, lapsing again to silence,
And all so dimly and so vague conceived
As is a shadowy unembodied thought
Yearning towards existence.
                                        Anon, the ripples
Of silvery waves on beach, faint musical peals,
The rustling shingle and soft sea-shells mixed;
The wind's small cymbals, grasses and river-reeds
Chafing together; the old elm-tree stirring,
The poplar spirit roused, forests awake,
The speechless heavens invoked, all things attent.

149

Now cries, most pitiful, most lamentable;
Sorrow, sorrow, sorrow; tears, all tears
Unutterable, from the soul in anguish wrung,
Wherein the hardest heart must find relief
Or melt in its own furnace. So ascends
The wail of innocents and outcast souls
Wandering through space, and so the wind intreats,
And imitates, on its poor instruments
Diviner griefs, deeper solicitudes.

Now sweetness, sweet, sweet, very sweet,
Sweeter than lilies, roses, violets,
All perfumes, odours, spices intermingled,
All dews, all unguents, and all essences,
Than milk and honey mixed, cordials and juices
Of purpling grapes, bruised leaves of briar and walnut,
Than the most melting string, divinely fingered,
Of lute or lyre harmoniously touched;
Than balm's own breath, than maiden's stolen kisses,
Than Summer's sickly incense, waters melodious
Over worn stones and pebbles; Spring's dulcet song,
Love's sugared supplement, sweet, most sweet.

Now riches, beauty, wealth, magnificence,
Rustlings of silks and satins, gorgeous apparel,
Gold, jewels, Indian pearl, and ornament;
Visions of cornfields, purple vintages,
Of mellowing pears and medlars, burnished Autumn,
Skies rich with sunset, crimson-shaded forests,
Emblazoned shields, and kingly circumstance,
In one slow, stately, measured pomp proceeding.

150

Now general laughter, joy, the marriage song,
Bells rapturously rung, feasting and revelry,
The strong breeze inland and the clapping waves,
The boisterous ocean and the loud applause,
Growing more momently, as the tempest quickens
O'er the incoming waters, sounds afar.

Now moanings, seas tempestuous, mutterings,
High altercation, trumpet sounds of war,
White-crested torrents, old Ocean's bottom moved,
And dreadful clouds low-stooping, thunder-hung.
Foam, foam, foam; the yawning dark abyss,
The deep tremendous and the cloud-capped height.

Now majesty, majesty, majesty,
Solemn and awful, death, and death, and death;
Ruin and earthquake shocks, the crashing shores,
Thunder's long roll, and lightning's vivid blaze;
The whole mass tottering, heaven and earth confused,
Hills shaking, crouching forests, cracking branches;
Sun, moon and stars removed; the prolonged roar
Of thunderous ocean's mighty cataracts,
Piling of mountainous seas on moles and piers,
Very destruction, very, very death.

Dawn, and the heavens' clear face; the distant peals
Receding, all the winds in rapid flight.
White streaks upon the water; echoes, echoes,
Fainter and fainter; bells; the stars twinkling;
Now again tears and sorrow's face renewed.
Now happy meadow scenes, tall woods and avenues;
The rain's sweet patter, gentle-murmuring leaves,
Sunset and evening calm, o'er-powering peace.

ASPIRATIONS.

I.

O Soul, thou uncreated,
Mystic, unimaginéd,
Unimaginable spirit,
With a mortal body mated,
Shapen to divine redress,
Passionate and passionless,
All-possessing, yet unsated,
Who dost all in all inherit;
Why, when all the world is waiting
Slumber-wise before the goal,
This divene exuberating?
Why fearest, and why tremblest,
What joy or grief dissemblest,
What rivers in thee roll?

II.

Can that which knows nor form nor mould
And older than the heavens are old,
Out-aging earth and sky,
That moveth over and beneath,
Nor tasteth food, nor draweth breath,
Unsubject to the bond of death,
Be ever brought to die?
From God the endless ages roll,
He wrought the body, breathed the soul,
We are the parts and He the whole,
And a part of Him am I:
Earth fadeth, and Time flieth,

Life liveth, and Death dieth,
Spring bloometh, Autumn staineth,
God giveth and God gaineth,
No other hope remaineth
But thou, Eternity!
Then chide not, soul, to wear thy fetter;
Gold is not wasted in the fire;
Soul bondage makes the soul aspire
To something nobler, something higher;
Desire attained is not desire;
Through ill we rise to better.

III.

Mystery of mysteries!
We shall change, but we shall not die;
We perish not who perish,
Some soil the seed will cherish
Though deep in the earth we lie;
The flowers that sicken in the breeze
And leaves that wither on the trees
Will blossom by and by;
Not we, but the earth around us,
The cloudy bonds that bound us
Will vanish utterly.
We shall dream, but we shall not sleep,
Waking we shall dream hereafter;
Age will sow, but Youth will reap
Riches wonderful and deep,
While our souls, vibrating, keep
Rippling with incessant laughter.

Nothing is that will not be;
All the Maker hath invented
Seeing, we shall truly see,
Not changed, but re-presented.
Youth wasteth, and Age calleth,
Day fleeteth, the night falleth,
Joy sateth, Beauty cloyeth,
Time runneth, not destroyeth,
Death freeth, not enthralleth.
O that high Wisdom would reveal
The power to create,
And trample with a mortal heel
The old offender, Fate!
Spoil Fortune of her iron wheel,
And set the burning stamp and seal
On Life immensurate!

IV.

By ceaseless constant motion
All things existent be;
And duty and devotion
Revolve eternally,
As the blue tide seeks the ocean
And the river seeks the sea;
By falls we rise to high emprise
And the hills of victory.
A brother for a brother
Sustains the toil and toll,
We live for one another,
As parts unto a whole;
One heart beats through and for us.

One hope exultant springs,
One heaven is opened o'er us,
One rest one comfort brings;
Through the valley of affliction,
Through sorrow and through strife,
We march to benediction,
And win the guerdon, Life.

IN MEMORIAM.

J. R. BIDDISCOMBE.

Not death, but slumber; virtue never dies;
   Therefore what need of unrequited tear?
He's gone, he's fled; he sleeps, and will arise;
   No earthly fetter could detain him here.

His life was gentle, as his soul was brave;
   Generous in action, feeling to the end;
Unseen he pitied, and unasked he gave,
   A loving husband and a faithful friend.

ON A LOST FRIEND.

And thou art dead!
   Closed be thy door!
Thy page is read,
   Thy task is o'er;
Across the sky
   The crescent bark
Of day passed by
   To after-dark.

No more the thrush
  To rapture grows,
A death-like hush
  Is on the rose;
One dewy tear,
  One sigh, one moan,
One grief to bear,
  The world alone.

The mother mourns
  Beside the cot,
The infant turns
  And knows thee not;
Upon the grass,
  With noiseless tread,
The neighbours pass,
  And name thee dead.

  *   *   *   *   *

Weave him no flower,
  Save such as grew
At twilight hour
  Dim in the dew;
Leaves red and brown
  Upon a cross,
Or careless crown
  Of scented moss.

Nor do you weep
  That he is gone;
Lo! as we sleep
  The hour steals on;

A breath, a space,
  A day, no more!
So soon the race
  Of Life is o'er.

Here we have met,
  We know not why;
Suns rise and set,
  And moons wane by,
Awhile we feed
  A tiny flame,
And dying speed
  To whence we came.

THE ROSE.

THERE'S a rose in the eve's sweet blush
  With an aureole,
And a crimson rose on the bush,
  And a rose in my soul;
The rose that's a-bloom in the West
  In Earth's garden grew,
But the rose that arose in my breast
  It drinketh of heavenly dew.

I doubt not but sweetness lives
  In the blossoming skies,
And the sweet that my garden gives
  Is like Love's surprise;
But O! that which breathes and distils
  From my soul's dear bloom
Is so sweet that it sweetens and fills
  Eternity with its perfume.

157

THE DEVOTEE.

Down where the great ship glideth
Mid purple-spouting waves,
And Ocean rudely chideth,
'Tis there my fancy hideth
In moonlight-haunted caves,
Seeking upon the opal-tinted floor
The ruddy gems that bloom and fade and bloom no more.

Where in the high noon shineth
The sacred silvery fane,
My spirit low reclineth
As a rose that droops and pineth
And thirsteth after rain,
Listening to catch the first faint breath that brings
The evening's sweet return with dew upon its wings.

Were I a cloud that spinneth
Its white threads in the air,
Where the blue heaven beginneth
And the sun its journey winneth
I'd mount, I know not where,
Leaving the pearly ocean-caves behind me
To revel with the spheres, where Thou alone could'st find me.

THE PURSUER.

Lo! in the world's dim hiding-place
I run, to shield me from thy face;
But, like a lightly rustling wind,
I hear thy foot-steps close behind.

Then down the frozen water-fall,
Where Nature's thunderous voices call,
I leap, amid the Soul's dark night;
But still Thou followest in the flight.

Now, rushing up the liquid air,
I seek the sun, but Thou art there;
Returning down Heaven's starry steep
I find Thee hovering in the deep.

Who art Thou that thyself dost hide
Amid the darkness at my side?
Or God, or Spirit; moving whence
To seal my soul's sad incidence?

Ah! from thy face how should I flee,
Or whither hide myself from Thee?
Now prostrate at thy feet I fall,
And willing answer to thy call.

MY SOUL IS FREE AS AMBIENT AIR.

My soul is free as ambient air,
  Although my body pinioned is;
The slave-born fetters that I wear
  Are dear companions of my bliss,

159

That lighten, while they still confound;
  Who wears the rose heeds not the thorn,
Small time will heal the quickest wound,
  And wrongs are milder smoothly borne.

The dearly-dreaded dissonance
  Of wolfish din and owlish cries
Fades to a low-lipped resonance,
  Sour speech to sweetest symphonies;

For, though my drooping spirit faints,
  And high Imagination falls
At hourly-idle cold complaints
  Wide-echoed round my prison walls,

The secret spring of poesy—
  The scented soul's divinest part—
Wells up and sweetens inwardly
  All the deep bitters of the heart.

Though I am in great company
  Yet walk I in deep solitude,
For plenty is in poverty,
  And famine in the multitude;

And when I am at duty's post
  I breathe an inward-deepening moan.
That, while I am attended most,
  Then do I languish most alone.

TO MY MOTHER.

My spirit seeketh thine,
And crieth sore
To clasp, and kiss, and twine,
And fold thee o'er and o'er.

O thou, my loved, my own!
I would not bide,
But flee, where thou art flown,
Though Death's dark stream divide.

For still before mine eyes
Thy form I see,
That ever flits and flies
And beckons unto me,

Calling me up and on,
Through heaven's wide space,
Where ever, round the sun,
The moons and stars embrace.

And I will follow thee
Where distant planets shine.
Till, in the immensity,
My spirit kisseth thine.

SAILING DOWN TO CAPE TOWN.

Ah! once more to be riding
Down the southern main,
And our proud ship gliding, gliding
O'er the unruffled plain,
When the depth of a dear delight was akin to mortal pain.

Again to see the splashing
Of the blue tide as it flows,
And the feathery foam-flakes flashing
In an iris from the bows;
When the morning sun was golden and the eve a mystic rose;

While, through the noon-tide gazing
Upon the lucid deep,
At beauty so amazing
My heart would bound and leap,
And question if my sense were waking or asleep.

Thus, ere the tempests quicken,
And the Fury howls and cries,
And winter sorrows thicken,
On cloud-wings I would rise
And journey through the deep to seek those sunny skies.

SAVING THE GUNS.

"Well get the guns back yet,"
  The gallant Grenfell said,
"The German host shall never boast
  That British Lancers turned and fled" -
The ground with his own blood was wet.

162

From centre, left, and right,
  The livid torrent came;
The bullets streamed, the bayonets gleamed,
  The very heaven was hot with flame,
And still more fiercely raged the fight.

The gunners, one and all,
  Lay stretched upon the ground;
With staring eyes fixed on the skies
  They died, but uttered not a sound:
They heard and answered Duty's call.

With Grenfell at their head
  The daring heroes dashed,
While through the mist the bullet hissed,
  And loud the noisy cannon crashed,
And burst in fury o'er the dead.

Hurrah! for Grenfell's deed,
  The guns are safe brought back!
Though wounded sore, the pain he bore,
  And calm pursued the bloody track
To gain the victor's glorious meed.

CROSSING THE MARNE.

"MAKE ready! make ready!" the Colonel cried,
  "The night is over and daw'ns at hand
Like blood in the east, and on every side
  The iron walls of the Prussian stand;
To the river's brim, where the barges swim,
  And the painted ferry-boats pitch and toss,
We'll up and away, ere the break of day,
  And force the enemy's troops across.

"Grasp each his rifle, for French has said —
  'Fight over the Marne,' and it's fight we will;
And though the river be choked with dead,
  And turned from its course, we'll not pause until
We have crossed the ford with fire and sword,
  In spite of all the withering guns,
Or bridged the flood and proudly stood
  On the height where the lordly river runs."

So they forward pressed and the morning came,
  Touching the hills with her finger-tips,
While the earth was tortured with shot and flame
  That leapt from the cannon's murderous lips;
The bullets fell, and the screaming shell
    Went slaughtering through them rank by rank
With a ghastly track, but they turned not back
  Till they reached the echoing river-bank.

Loud shrieked the shrapnel, the rifles spat;
  Crash! went girder, buttress and beam;
Wounded and dying sprawled, huddled, or sat;
  Rider and horse sank into the stream:
The gun-smoke showed like a thundercloud,
  And hung o'er woodland, valley, and tarn,
And the ground was red, but the foe had fled,
  And the British were safe across the Marne.

AFTER THE BATTLE.

WHEN the battle-cloud is lifting,
And the loud guns cease to roar,
And the stately ship goes drifting
Back unto her native shore,
Many a weary heart will sorrow, sifting
Thoughts of the noble dead that come not evermore.

When, amid the desolation
Of the thunder-riven plain,
Cities ring with exultation
At the end of blood and pain,
Nought can bring the happy consolation
To those whose hopes are shattered and whose tears are vain.

Till the stars' gold light is failing
In the memory-haunted room,
And the purple east is paling,
Cometh ever through the gloom
A sound as of a low wind sadly wailing —
The loved one's lonely spirit prisoned in the tomb.

TO BRITAIN AT THE PEACE CONFERENCE. 1919.

MOTHER of heroes, valiant and wise,
In whom all hope of highest freedom lies.
Bind not the fetter on thyself, nor yield
Weakly to what the impotent devise.

Lo! fools and sages in the city meet,
The strong man urges and the cowards bleat;
For all seduction look thou not aside,
For Fate will her old prophecy repeat.

Then wert thou feeble didst thou promise make
No more in justice thy strong arm to shake,
While plotting peoples compass thee about
And of thy pride their petty vengeance take.

From age to age the living record runs,
And stays not with the process of the suns;
By deep subversion Truth is stabilised,
And Freedom lives with the all-shattering guns.

After the midnight storm the calm dawn breaks,
As out of death all new existence wakes;
There's no disaster worthy of the name,
And forward still Success her journey takes.

Out of thy scattered dust henceforth shall rise
Nations more strong, more daring, and more wise,
And, strength to strength opposing, recreate
The world, growd weary of her long demise.

VI.

SONNETS

TO LORD FITZMAURICE.

I

FITZMAURICE, as some veteran of the race,
  Who, all life long contending, heart and soul,
  Shunning the proffered bribe and secret dole,
Battling the winds of fortune face to face,
With eyes hard set, and firm, unflinching pace,
  Round whom the thunderous acclamations roll,
  Who, thinking swiftly to attain the goal,
By some mischance has lost the foremost place;
So, when the laurel crown was barely won,
  And those large honours certain merits yield.
  When Fame's high gate stood open and revealed,
Life's strenuous battle sternly fought and done,
Low in the beams of the departing sun
  Stricken thou liest in the tented field.

II.

What is thy guerdon then, who long hast stood
  Proud in the wearing of a spotless name,
  Unshaken by the fickle crowd's acclaim,
With Freedom's noblest passion deep endued?
This; that thy care was of the multitude;
  That, while some men have cast about for shame,
  Thou hast continued free from taint or blame,
For ever mindful of the common good:
Therefore, be strengthened with this virtuous thought,
  And often to thyself this comfort tell: —
  "If, in my country's cause, I blameless fell,
Thus to an end my toils untimely brought,
So be it! Time has witnessed that I wrought;
  Happy who falls and perishes, fighting well".

169

TO EDWARD SLOW. (Wilton.)

Edward, whatever hence shall be thy lot,
  Whether thou lingerest in thy decline,
  Or thy presuming fates too soon combine
To wrench thee from this dear and flowery spot;
However this shall be, it matters not,
  Be sure, the breath and spirit of thy line,
  Apart from any eulogy of mine,
Will serve thee, thou wilt never be forgot!
My right good wishes for thy safety, friend!
  And whosoever, when the curfew chimes,
  Sitting at ease, shall read thy merry rhymes,
Threading the humorous page from end to end,
Let him with sympathetic heart attend
  And bless the memory of the good old times.

STONEHENGE.
I.

Mystery unbreathable! Beyond compare!
  Plain, naked, stately, simple, yet sublime;
  Faith's eldest progeny, got in the prime
Of her connubial season, standing there
Sensibly silent, movers of despair,
  The very index and the mark of Time,
  Bare to the rigours of a changeful clime,
To the inclemencies of wind and air:
So huge of structure and of bulk so vast,
  So firm in ruin, mighty in decay,
  Magnificently steadfast in array,
It seems your thunder-stricken sides will last
Till hill and valley, storm and flood be past,
  And Earth's foundations fall and melt away.

II.

Speak, you dumb stones! Open your mouths: proclaim
  Your congregated secrets, for it must be
  That you have noted much. Say! whence are ye,
And wherefore? How long is it that ye came?
Under what period, and in whose name
  Ye were established? Who, and what was he,
  What power, what demon, god, Divinity
Favoured your altar? Answer back the same.
For ye are able, haply if ye will,
  To satisfy this craving, and ye must
  Deliver it, or be forever thrust
Into the womb of Silence, and fulfil
Time's fixéd penalty, sinking deeper still
  Into Oblivion's enduring dust.

III.

But ye are silent, harking not the call;
  Your speechless mouths no known responses yield;
  Your stone-blind eyes look vacant o'er the field,
Your sides are crusted like the mountain-wall;
Your grizzled features frighten and appal,
  Wherein is utter hopelessness revealed,
  Your hearts are passionless, your lips are sealed,
Ye sleep and wake not, answer not at all.
Above, the sky looks down, day after day,
  The rosy morning's maiden blush of shame,
  The intenser noon, and evening's ruddy flame;
The distant hill-top rises, bare and grey,
The solitary Downs stretch wide away,
  All things continue, ye are still the same.

171

IV.

Poor stones, I pity you! Poor, senseless things!
  Poor human relics of a day long-sped!
  Poor offspring of an age deceased and dead,
Round whom impenetrable mystery clings!
Disconsolate children! not an hour but brings
  Strong Desolation's proof, and Ruin dread
  Shoots all her bolts and arrows at your head,
Around, the melancholy tempest rings.
How would that venerable architect,
  Of rugged science, nameless and untold,
  With quickening concept, sorrow to behold
His massy piers, with many an offering decked,
His universal temple stormed and wrecked,
  His fires extinguished, and his altars cold!

V.

Methinks whoever would immortalise
  These deathless monuments — if such there be
  In this round universe — such a one as he
Would scorn the baser element and rise
Reckless to Heaven, the hollow earth despise,
  Call Bondage circumscribed, and Freedom free,
  Would seek to immortalise Immortality,
And bring Jove's stature down to pigmy size;
For they are Time's own heritage, bequeathed
  To late posterity, his immortal part,
  Whence thought, whence knowledge, all inquiry start,
With Memory's ornaments entwined and wreathed;
Time's spirited symbol, imperishably breathed
  Out of the depths of his almighty heart.

172

SALISBURY CATHEDRAL.

I.

WHO shall enliken thee? Who shall compare
  Thy consummate majesty? What rash soul would deem
  To express thee, far beyond the poet's theme,
Save that immortal soul's who fixed thee there,
A nameless singer? Who in verse so rare
  Would point the inference of thy walls, that seem
  The spiritual inflorescence af a dream,
The echo of a heavenly chanted air?
Let him be silent, or if he must break
  The hallowed stillness with superfluous tongue—
  Poor in his feebleness, though ne'er so strong—
Let him at least this premonition take,
His muse will but subjective music make
  Of that which far transcends all powers of song.

II.

HARK! 'tis the organ's muffled note that steals
    Soft as a summer echo on our ears,
    More faintly distant than the moving spheres,
  The musical rumbling of low-sounding wheels,
  Growing more momently; now like wind-borne peals
    Wafted at eventide, when high up appears
    Bright golden Hesperus; now the thunder nears
  Till the stupendous fabric shakes and reels:
  Soon the loud tempest falls away and dies,
    Rustling like lotus leaves or quaking palm,
    Lapsing to silence and a breathless calm;
  When from the stilness other sounds arise,
  And all the full-voiced company replies
    Great with the holy Israelitish psalm.

173

III.

NAY! here thy stone is something out of place;
  Thou should'st be throned and seated out-of-doors
  On thy lone hill-top, where the skylark soars,
And fleeting swallows ply the dizzy race,
Where gold-winged butterflies join in the chase,
  And that loud-trilling thrush his music pours,
  Or where the wintry tempest madly roars,
Dashing his bitter drops against the face.
There thou should'st stately sit, superb, supine,
  Fearless against the North's unkindly blast,
  Whether the heaven were clear or overcast,
Musing with that prophetic soul of thine
Till thou should'st scale a summit more divine
  And come to thine inheritance at last.

IV.

O that I were an Architect! I would build
  In lasting marble to thy name, as high
  As the entrancing clouds, beneath a sky
Of rainbow brightness, with Joy's feature filled,
On thy beloved Down-lands, gentle-hilled,
  Forever in the sun's all-seeing eye,
  Round which the feathered host of heaven should fly,
Where Nature's music never should be stilled:
And I would sculpture it with leaves and flowers,
  And loving chaplets should thy brow adorn
  Of fragant meadow-sweet and golden corn;
There Youth and Beauty, with replenished powers,
Should bloom perpetual with the laughing Hours,
  And Plenty wield her inexhaustible horn.

174

V.

Ah! let us leave him here! Let us depart!
  Yet I will think of him in after time,
  Weaving my barren thought in thankless rhyme
Far from Cyclopean Labour's booming mart;
And, if a feeling tear do sudden start,
  Musing of him, whose painful soul did climb
  Affliction's ladder to a height sublime,
Not from the eye it streams, but from the heart;
For I have suffered, too, Grief's piercing stings,
  And oft have sighed Health's blooms and roses blown,
  In my heart's chamber uttering groan on groan.
O God! how tight the mortal fetter clings!
Jefferies! the bitter pangs Experience brings
  Have cleft my soul asunder with thine own.

TO THE POET HERBERT.
BEMERTON CHURCH.
I.

WHAT though no monumental marbles rear
  Their sculptured crowns 'mid the pervading gloom,
  Nor outward ornament deck the inner tomb,
Whose lowly stone is graven with many a tear!
What if no funeral pomp or show appear,
  No flowers of Art, spreading an endless bloom!
  The air is fragrant whit his soul's perfume;
The Holy of Holies is anointed here:
So let him rest beneath the hallowed wall,
  Lulled by the music of the vesper bell
  Till the last trumpet sound of doom shall swell!
Here let Heaven's curtain o'er eyelids fall
Till he shall quicken at the final call,
  In this dim sanctuary he loved so well!

II.

Clear through the chancel casement as of yore
    On sacramental cross, at break of day,
    Still do the crimson-rosy sunbeams play
Where the divine musician stood before;
At even, scattered from the western floor,
  The glimmering sunlight, where oft-times it lay,
  Lingers a moment, and then dies away,
But that long-wished-for step returns no more:
High up the wall the verdant ivy creeps;
  Around, the rough-hewn monuments are spread
  The branching cedar lifts her slender head,
Shy through the grass the modest violet peeps.
And ah! within, the poet-prophet sleeps
The last long dreamless slumber of the dead.

SONNET IN AUTUMN.

Hark! through the tree-tops comes a rustling sour
  That sets my strained and anxious heart athrill
  With its intensity, and louder still,
Till thud! upon the bosom of the ground;
Sudden I spring, and cast an eye around,
  And overlook the margin of the hill,
  And through the inner shades and glooms that
The hollow valley to the deep profound.
Nothing! Far off the languid shepherd wends
  To summon up his flocks, the labouring swain
  Toils in the furrow and the shadows stand.
What, then? A chestnut fell; the fall portends
Summer's o'er-hasty death, September's wane,
  And Winter, waiting to possess the land.

176

ON THE ROAD TO BAYDON.

How still, how solitary are the heights
 That round me in a sweeping circle lie!
 A hazy texture intercepts the sky,
The glimmering field is strewed with golden lights;
The languorous air to soothing sleep invites;
 No breath to mar the stillness, not a sigh!
 No rustling cricket's chirp, nor any cry,
No peewits wheeling their aerial flights.
It seems that every living thing were fled;
 Suspended Nature hung aside her lute;
That ghostly Silence, from the land of dread,
 Stole hitherward our senses to confute;
That the inhabitable world were dead;
 Language unheard of, sound itself were mute.

THE ROMAN RUINS AT CHEDWORTH.

HERE once the Roman minstrel piped and sung;
 The dexterous blacksmith plied his iron trade;
 The busy looms their warp and woof displayed;
The old centurion's sword and buckler hung;
War's brazen implements aside were flung;
 Now tuned the midnight songstress in the glade;
 The fluttering eagle cast a peaceful shade:
The timid maiden to her lover clung:
I hear the music clashing in the halls;
 Shrilly the *tibia* sounds, and louder yet
The lusty trumpet peals, the clarion calls,
 Briton and Roman, king and conqueror met;
Now blooms the wild flower 'mid the crumbling walls,
 Nature's own seal upon the ruin set!

THE OLD YEAR.

'Tis but a step to midnight; one stroke more,
  One fleeting space for sorrows and farewells,
  One last look backward where high Memory dwells,
Then in the untrodden path that lies before
We must push onward, ever to that shore
  Towards which our utmost fate draws and compels;
  Hark! from the starlit tower the merry bells
Peal as they've pealed a thousand times of yore.
All this is banished, whether good or ill;
  Our joys and sufferings, our toils and pains
  Diminish, our life's star waxes and wanes.
Ere the dark wave close o'er us, deep and still,
Let us arise, fearless in mind and will,
  And grapple with the future that remains.

THE DEPARTURE. 1914.

The ships go forth, majestic on the wave,
  Bearing their precious sum of human freight,
  Bound to a port unknown. In towering state
The Ocean-Sentinels, to guard the brave,
Stood mute, and silent approbation gave;
  Britannia rose and opened wide her gate,
  While half her sons, lured with a blood-red fate,
Swept proudly through to glory or the grave.
Happy is Britain, Freedom's surest friend,
  That nobly, for her honour's sovereign sake,
  Bares her bright sword -to stem the foe's advance!
Now the swift ships swim towards the harbour's end,
  Where, from the shore, the joyful thunders break,
  And England leaps into the arms of France.

RIGHT INVIOLATE. 1914.

WHAT! is it thus? What! this the end, the doom?
  Shatters the thunder; fierce the lightning gleams,
  Flash unto flash; Earth's panting bosom seems
Lit with the splendour of a blood-red bloom.
O God our help! Is this the grave, the tomb
  Of hopes long-hoped, our fondest, surest dreams?
  Is Justice thwarted by a madman's schemes?
Shall Freedom's sun set low in deepest gloom?
Never for ever! 'Tis decreed by Fate
  Who strikes at Freedom shall go reeling down
  To ruin, big with loss of all his sons.
The end's not yet. Lo! Right inviolate
  Unshaken sits on her Heaven-guarded throne,
  And Truth peals louder than the battle guns.

TO ONE.

Anxious that the poet should forbear to write of war
  and sing only of pastoral joys and sylvan peace.

TALK not of peace. Dear God! who once would sleep
  On primrose-studded banks by brake or dell
  Dreaming of Paradise, while War's loud bell
Clangs dismal, and its thunder shakes the deep?
While earth is piled with many a quivering heap,
  And skies are rent with bursting shot and shell,
  Who would forget the horrors of that hell,
Or suffer Beauty on his soul to creep?
Sweet is the morning hour and sweet the eve.

179

The song of birds, the dew upon the grass—
All nature exquisite with leaf and bloom;
But grinning Death persists and will not leave
His orgies. Stir thy spirit, till thou pass
The Crisis, heavy with a people's doom.

BRITAIN'S HEROES.

Weep not for Britain's heroes. Wherefore shed
    Tears, when ye know that all is safe and well?
    Glorious their lot, and proud their fate who fell
Fighting for Freedom, and bowed not the head
At the Insulter's will. They are not dead,
    But living beautiful; this Time shall tell.
    Loud sound the Triumph! Let the pean swell!
Weep not, but crown yourselves with flowers instead,
Great is their fame, Eternity their prize—
    For Glory, blushing Virtue's brightest bloom,
Fades not, nor withers unto endless days—
Who reaped Remembrance in the place of sighs;
    For sorrow, Joy; an Altar for a tomb;
    Laughter for tears; instead of pity, Praise.

THE TESTAMENT

I.

Come, you oak trees and hazels, you old-fashioned elms and beeches,
You shrunk and shaded pool, with the willows and the maples,
The loving boughs and branches and the hawthorn still beside it.
With the sweetened scent of summer, breathing gentle and delicious.
Let us gather all together where no other eye can see us,
In the densely crowded shadow, with the heifer and the yearling.
Twine our arms and sit together with the music all around us.
And listen to the murmurs of the distant world beyond us.
You know I could not tarry long without you, I am tired of streets and
    faces.
When I walk between the high walls with the crowd pushing at my
    elbow,
The old and young and middle-aged, laughing and talking together.
That seem to be in love with their prison, almost enraptured with it;
Or see them walking up and down, now pausing to gaze in a window.
Now standing in several groups, solemnly conversing and discussing
The last phase of the moon, or something or other of a scandal,
Or trooping from the theatre and hall, or the room political.
Flushed with extreme success, or pale with disappointment.
Observing the powdered features of the dames, with the florid ornament,
And the studied appearance of the males, the youths and the gentlemen,
The gross ring on the finger, the hair most carefully brushed and divided,
And that high and haughty look, as good as "I am the emperor,"
Then my heart grows dead within me, my spirits droop, I despair of
    myself,
I long to escape to the little wooded glen, or field with the cattle grazing.
Or hide myself in the old forked willow over the stream,
Or else throw my arms round the trunk of a spreading oak-tree.
Or stand concealed in the hazels, and listen to the birds in the roof
    overhead.
Or peer into the rounded nest with the sky-blue eggs, and black spots
    upon them,
Or wander up and down the cornfield with the green waves rippling.
The skylark singing in the clouds above, and the pale-blue butterflies.
The ground ivy under my feet, and the pink and white convolvulus.

Or, failing this, if I am not too tired and over-weary,
Too beaten and distressed with circumstance, with the day's adventure.
My soul cries for the long sloping hill, perched above the valley.
The delicate curving hill, the old ancient inheritance,
The loving sisterly hill, the purifying hill, the windswept tabernacle.
With the carved and runic feature of the rampart and the gully,
The gold glamour of thorn-broom, the dwarfed and stunted heather.
And that delicious life-giving breath, blowing continually,
Strong with immortality— I can perceive it in my nostrils,
I know every time I inhale it, and constantly affirm it to myself,
That having once drunk the elixir, the draught electrical,
It is useless for Death to lay his frigid cold hand upon me —
So, coming back to you once more — as a sailor from sea returning —
Make haste to welcome me all with your loving, fond caresses,
While I sit in the shelter of you here, and warble out a melody.

II.

There is nothing very delectable in that I would sing to you,
You have heard it all before, there is no need to name you anything.
Other lips before mine have sung, you have had your mouthpieces,
You are yourselves the song, I am no more than an instrument.
Lo! a chord is struck within me, I echo forth, the note expands, reiterates.
Again I become silent, the string of life is broken, mutilate.
I pass to the great majority, or I am cast aside like a vestment.
Fools! I laugh in your faces, I pour out my ridicule upon you,
Thinking to be so lightly quit of me, or of yourselves, I will cling to you;
I yield my corporal body back to earth, but the song continues.
You know the cruelty and unkindness of men, you will not forget it,
How they scorned the breath of my mouth, and very nearly laid hands
    upon me,
How they hated one of your children— and one of theirs — and stepped
    aside quickly.
Now covertly waiting in the distance, taking slow note of my footsteps.
Now using all manner of complaints, and worthless poor objections.
Rejoicing to see me pierced and bruised with sorrows, and stung with
    reproaches.

I do not blame them for it, it is not theirs, they are the sufferers;
I am too strong for envy, I know myself that I am not impotent.
I can bear my burden cheerfully, and smile under it, I do not exalt myself.
I have no desire of riches, nor of honour, I enjoy all naturally;
I am the heir of all that I see, that is my possession;
And the things that are invisible and eternal are mine also.
I can count the wind in particles, I can reason with it from the hill-top.
The clouds of sweetness arising from the earth and the flowers, the scents,
    and odours.
And catch the streaming flood of song poured from a thrush's throat or
    a skylark's —
How broadly it is carried out! How it shoots and thrills and penetrates!
How it winds and undulates, and ripples up and down in waves and
    filaments!
All this I embody in my song, I have learned it of my parent.
I have had no school but my own thoughts, no other pedagogue,
But several books for my tutors, my own staff to lean upon.
I am not anxious to please any, nor yet desirous of offending any;
I can kneel with humanity, or soar with them, I am not above them.
I am bound by no rule of flesh and blood, no covenants and compacts;
Treaties are no more in my eyes than the written bonds of disagreement.
If I have wronged any man I am sorry for it, I no more apologise;
If there is any satisfaction arising from it, it is due to myself;
The pain of punishment is greater in me than in him I have injured;
There is no hell greater than that of a guilty conscience.

III.

It is good to be with you at all times, not in spring or summer only;
To sit in the shelter of you and hear your song, that is my condition.
To me all times and seasons are alike, if there is any difference, it is in
    myself;
One moon is as good as another to me, and May no more beautiful than
    December.
Age was not always old; December had a husband once;
Nothing is stable long, and May will one day be a widow.
One praises Spring. That is natural. It is the season of hope, adorable.

I myself am in love with it. I am happy with the green earth and the
 flowers arising,
The slant rays of the sun, the sweetness and the song, the young lambs
 bleating.
I could sit all day, and all night in the stars, I am never weary of it.
This, more passionate, awaits the time of June and the roses,
A foretaste is not enough, he must deeply revel in it,
He must know the rich grass up to his knees, all things a-ripening;
The corn yellowing in the valley, or on the hill, the trees laden with fruit,
The little stream very nearly dried up, the earth tormented.
The day drawn out to the uttermost, the night abridged, almost
 annihilated.
All this I fully appreciate, it is mine as well as his, I am drunk with the
 exuberance of it,
I am happy with a little, or I can admire much; I do not covet anything.
Another, more riotous and intense, smacks his lips at Autumn;
For him the purple vintage, the golden corn, and the olives,
The thresher at his work, the wains plying and returning.
The long ladder trailing in the orchard, or the pear tree by the chimney,
The golden russets here, the queen pippin, or the seedling,
The late plum waiting to be delivered, the bullace and the damsons,
The brown cobs, and the hazels, the chestnuts, and the filberts,
The hedges groaning under their weight, each ready with an offering.
Earth with her crowded arms, and none able to receive it.
I grant every man his right and his pleasure, I am not niggardly.
Let him be satisfied; for that is the aim of all life, and a great part happiness.
I am temperate in all things, and at all times, I praise none excessively;
For me the shadow and cloud are no less than the sunlight;
They have their uses and equivalents; I am no judge, I submit myself.
All delights meet and blend in me, all climates, conditions;
I drink my fill of them all, and rejoice that I am not another.
The grey twilight pleases me, the intense noon, or the still evening;
I praise the birth, and the death, the end, and the beginning.
I am at one with them all, I am raging as well as peaceful;
I can be calm or perturbed, I follow Nature in all things; I was born
 natural,

I can enjoy a tempest, I love to hear the wind howling.

I can hear myself in it, as soon as it arrives, I go forth, expedient,

I stand on the hill, or under the oaks. How it roars, precipitates!

I turn my face to it and draw deep breaths, I open my arms, I embrace
— myself!

Higher and higher I raise my head; now the rain sweeps in torrents
deliciously.

Full on my forehead it beats and runs down, there is more than sweetness
in it.

I leave the shelter of the oaks, I go forward. Now the clouds come down.

The hills are hid with a coverlet, and the valley also, I am very nearly
hid myself,

I pass the yearlings, and the heifer great with calf, they look up at me;

I pause and comfort them, now they advance, they put out their nostrils
inquiringly;

I can feel the dew of their breath; now they touch my hand; I pass on.

Here are no cutting words, all kindness; still the wind increases.

This is no mortal feeling; I do not fear now; my faith grows; I defy
everything.

Here is another oak, not so large. Again I pause. I put an arm around it.

Yonder is the wood. Crash the wind takes it. I feel myself lifted up.

Was ever music like it? Ever the sea, so lofty, majestical?

Now, greater than myself, I draw near to the wood, I crouch very low,
I enter in.

Within, all is dark. I become entangled; still the rain beats heavily.

I am wet with the moisture. I look up, there is no heaven visible,

Only the wildly tossing boughs, the loud orchestra, and the anthem
pealing.

The earth trembles, and the air trembles. My heart leaps. I cry out aloud.

Now cautious I thread my way to the light, the battle still proceeding.

Now I emerge again, I stand upright, this time delivered.

The oaks rain their acorns upon me, I gather some up and depart.

Now the storm weakens, and the wind. It is enough. I am strengthened
with it.

Now I go on my way, and grow back to life, leaving the tempest behind
me.

187

IV.

O dear-loving trees, my comrades, artistic and natural!
Now I feel my soul again gushing up like a river to come to you,
And a strange longing comes over my flesh, I feel mighty and strong,
I could press you for ever in my arms, like lovers in ecstasy.
And pour out the kisses like wine from my lips, overwhelm you with
    kindness,
I could make you my habitation and my temple, my very sweet dwelling,
I could sleep in the chamber of your leaves deliciously,
And wake to the music of them in the dew of the twilight;
I could dispense with all raiment and food, I could break my fast with
    you,
We could grow together in unity and love, and no friend should sever us;
I would talk with you in your own tongue, and you respond to me in
    the same.
We would scatter our affections equally on all around us;
Together we could see the old sun rise, and lift up our arms to him,
We could take his kindness to us and wave our leaves in his honour,
And give him a departing sign in the evening, when the dew arises;
The loving cattle would come to us in the long noon, and lie down gently,
Or stand crowded together, rejoicing to be so well consorted;
The wandering rook and the jay would seek us for embraces,
Above, the fond skylark would pour out his love upon us.
And that loud-warbling blackbird pursue us with his melody.
We should be deeply sated with song, yet never weary of it.
Always hungering for the same food, and always satisfied with it,
The same passions and feelings, the same hopes and fulfilments,
The same inward love and sympathy for men and things, prayers and
    devotions,
All the books of the earth lying wide open at our feet.
Full of divine pictures of beautiful things created;
Woven sweetness of flowers, precious jewels for possession,
Most careful and cunning patterns ef silks, and royal rich embroidery;
All shades and figures, all hues and dyes, pleasing to the eyesight,
And everything living, nothing without a soul and spirit in it,
Every page stamped with the perfect image of ourselves,

Wearing also the person of the Creator, his index and character;
Or, if we desire knowledge of a greater skill and compass.
There are the heavens to be looked at, like a written scroll over us,
Full of old signs and characters of letters and languages.
From the beginning eternal, and to the end eternal;
We could watch the evening star come up out of the valley.
Or that round orb of the moon, full of tears and penitence.
Rising like a city, and slow-stealing in the element;
Together we could rejoice in the delirious draughts of sunshine,
Or deeply drink in the perennial sweetness of showers and dews
    assembling;
The old wind would ruffle us, we would toy with him provokingly.
We would shed our round fruits one by one tenderly in Autumn,
And shake our leaves over them for a bed and a covering;
The timid conies would come to us, the speckled thrush would come to
    us.
The young boys looking for berries and fruits would smile at us cheerfully.
The old mare with the young foal would visit us with kindness.
And the green ivy cling to us frantically all the year through together;
The glittering hoar-frost would bestrew us with diamonds,
And the white snow wind itself round us in wreaths and mantles like
    wool;
We would sleep in the long nights, profoundly through the darkness,
And afterwards wake with a passion greater than all words, more
    devoted than ever,
That neither death, nor periods of time, nor eternity itself
Could ever rive or separate in us, so dearly we would love, and so truly.

V.

Now for a moment I leave you, here I desert you utterly.
I have already drunk you up. I am full to the brim. I am become riotous.
The stream of love overflows, the flood is in my soul, I tremble all over.
I stretch out an arm, I put a foot forward, I am lost, bewildered.
I feel myself all over down to the feet, but I am not in it.
The flesh is revealed, heated and passionate, that is not what I want.
It is myself I am looking for. Where is the small uniformity?

Where is the little divine something, that sure, pent-up image of myself?
Where is the beginning and end, the present and future of me?
The little, bright light ever burning continually?
Again I ask, with love and fear increasing, and put my whole soul in it;
Stand near to me, and answer if you can; tell we what and where I am.
Round and round I walk, this way and that, up and down fearfully.
Now I run for happiness. I skim over the green turf, now I end abruptly.
I see one pale star in the blue arising, but that is not myself.
Now I come to a pool. I bend over cautiously. I see a reflection in it;
That is my familiar, and I welcome it, but that is not myself.
Now I stoop to the ground, now I go forward again, I am discovered;
I am unseen still, I stand aside, the leaves and branches cover me.
Now the light breaks. Suddenly I cry out. I have solved the mystery.
I have found out what was lost, it was hidden all the time, and I never
    knew it.
I am that little something. *I* am the ingraven image, *I* am myself.
Now I go forward hopefully. I will tell the whole world of it.
Nature shall hear it, and man also. I will shout it triumphantly till my
    death.
I will remember my strength and my weakness, and tell myself very often
    what I am.
I will be true to myself henceforth, and for ever eternally.

VI .

O earth! O paradise! O flesh and blood! O quivering mortality!
O green-robed children of a parent full-begotten!
So loving and sisterly, so pure and passionate, overwhelming with desire
    of me.
Featured like myself, contemplative also, unsolicitous.
Lovers of solitude, yet not wholly retiring, giving and receiving,
Pushing your thoughts in blades and leaves, in lines and sentences,
Concealing in your hearts the written record of many seasons,
But chiefly the kindlers and augmentors of my flame and spirit,
I will not be long absent from you, I will return speedily,
I will fly in my love and my fear, I will rush upon you,
I will run breathlessly up the hill to you, I will call to you in the distance,

I will wave my hand to you, and you will wave your boughs back to me,
I will smile at you from afar, I shall cry out with joy, you will hear it and
answer,
You will catch the breath of my lips, and clap your leaves together;
O joy insupportable! O rapture beyond words! O ecstasy!
The virtue of reward, the toil forgotten, and the heaviness.
I render account to humanity, I could not wholly abide with them.
My heart would very soon be withered, and my soul also, I should be
quite dried up.
I should fade in their presence, I should droop like leaves, I should fall to
the earth,
I should lie scattered and dead, I should pine away in the solitude of
numbers,
I should be starved with plenty, I should be sick with fulfilment,
I should cry out secretly, I should long to run and hide myself,
I should think of all that is past, of my own tears, and the future yet to
come,
Of my youth and childhood, my age and my infancy;
I should look out with large full eyes, and turn them inwardly on myself;
There is no peace in life, it is not joy to be comfortable;
And to be satisfied with anything is worse than all diseases and deaths.
I myself will not rest, I will not lie down meekly.
I will arise like a giant, and shake myself; I will proudly lift up my head.
I will swear an oath to myself, and call all things in earth to my witness.
Never to rest while my heart beats on this side death, never to be humbled.
I will excel in my labour, I will leave nothing unfinished,
I will understand myself before I die, and this round frame, I will search
deeply.
I will chisel my name — how small soever — in the rock, I do not fear
greatness;
I can look into it, and above it if I will, there is nothing greater than life.
I will prove to them all, and pour out the fire of my contradiction,
I will return them the lie, and mountains of reproaches with it.
Beauty is not dead. Why! Earth is more adorable than ever.
Now is the time to be natural; the old Parent calls, everything is in
readiness.

The flowers bloom, and the woods ring; the hills are green with verdure,
the balm arises.
The milk flows, the honey is gathered, the small wind blows languidly.
The bees are flitting, and the butterflies, the sky is blue overhead.
The old star is genial, the air invites, there is dew in the distance.
The little stream murmurs under the arch, the corn waves in the valley,
The scythe is in the grass, the old labourer rests in the shadow.
The young colts rear playfully, the mother with her calf lies down gently.
The swain whistles, the team moves lazily. O the joy and beauty of it!
It is time to come forth. O, leave your cells and your cloisters;
Leave your painted prisons, your hovels of wood and masonry;
Leave your streets and pavilions, your dark dens and caverns,
Your homes and workshops, the noise of wheels and machinery;
Throw down the idols of debate! Put all care through the window.
What is the use of bubble and excitement, you have parleyed too long
already.
The sun rises and sets, the moon wanes and increases, the stars come out.
What is amiss must be sought nearer, Look in your own hearts. Nature
is natural.

VII.

O my beloved! I fear my cry is not heard. Let it not be made in vain.
Let not the little thread of song become abortive in me.
Let it go forth bravely, winding and undulating.
Let it come to fit ears, let it obtain sympathy.
There is no sweetness in it. It is not very acceptable.
I have heard richer sounds, I have looked in pools deeper with thought.
I have seen art so transfigured there was no art perceptible in it.
I have seen many shrines and temples, far greater than my own; that is
not my fault.
I have seen glorious toils of heroes and kings assembled.
I have seen murders and crimes, storms, and treasons committed.
I have been present at battles; I have seen the death of empires.
I have seen the sea red with blood, and ships in the deep descending.
I have seen the smoke of cities going up, and the chains of the vanquished.

I have marched through deserts and over mountains, I have heard the
trumpet pealing.
I have known the steady tramp of feet, and the loud drums, with the
cymbals;
All this immortalized in song; my own is very poor beside it.
Let it go forth the same, it is all sincerity.
It may meet some soul on its way, or come to earth finally.
All is not so changed, some few are translated.
There are the loiterers still, the steady procession.
The pillars of Opinion, the approved minority.
These are the kindred spirits, the salt of the earth, the dear rewarded.
Let my song come to them, let it fall on their ears faintly like an echo;
Let the wind drift it slowly like a cloud, let the waves of time bear it up;
Or let it not be heard at all, let it die down within me;
Let it be slowly strangled, let my soul be composed, and I at rest with it.
I have tried to be silent; I have sealed my lips; I have sworn secrecy;
I have given up all hope of myself, and walked in strange places:
But my heart opened higher than my lips, I could not contain the impulse;
I will go on till my death; I will follow and continue.
I have drawn a strange breath, I have smelt life with my nostrils,
I have imbibed secrets, I have drunk at the well of mystery;
I have seen Beauty playing with her sisters under the trees in the meadows.
And naked Love, purer than a lily, bathing in the sunlight.
I have played with Echo in the woods, I have dealt in herbs and simples;
I know where the East gathered her blush, and the West her brightness.
I know the breath of the South, why it is balmy, and sweet, and odourous;
And why the North is dreary and bleak, full of powders and crystals.
I know where the spring of Hope gushes out, and the fountain of song
arises,
There will I stoop with the cup of my lips, I will drink it up purely;
I will live in the world of my thought, in the palace of my imagination;
I will sing my song triumphantly, whether the world heed it or not, there
is duty in it.
I will finish the race; I will work my task. Be strong, O my soul, for
another

VIII .

Let everything living bear its own fruit openly, and conceal nothing.

Let the young grass grow in the field; let the green wheat wave in the
valley or on the hill-top.

Let the wild primrose bloom profusely under the willows and hazels;

Give space to the sweet violet, let her shame the woods with humility;

Let her revel in her own soul; soil not the temple of her virginity.

Let the blackthorn bloom in a cloud when the first of Spring arises;

Gather the starry daisies, and the dear, sweet buttercups;

Tenderly with the cowslips, they have braved the battle of winter, hail
them victorious;

Love the woods for blue-bells, treasure them for anemones;

Let the hyacinths deck the valley, let them follow on the daffodils.

Let the young sorrel spread its juicy sweet leaves, and the cuckoo-flowers.

Let the budding hawthorn bloom, let it veil the bush with drapery;

And let the air around be heavy with perfume, thick with the odours of it.

Let the rosy wild apple-blossom soar in towers and pyramids,

And the snowy-sweet alder, heavy and rich, gather on the bough in
clusters.

Welcome the dewy clover, and the purple pea. Love the delicate bean,
drink her in deeply.

O the bewildering soul of the bean, the divine sweet fragrance, the
breathing beauty of it!

Cherish the tender buds of the wild briar, watch the transformation;

Let them open and bloom, let them burst their cells, let them come forth
beautifully;

Let them swell and expand, and breathe their immaculate souls out
purely;

Let them fill heaven and earth with sweetness like a song, like a cloud
arising;

Let the tender wood-lilies bloom, pale and demure, like beautiful young
maidens;

And the trailing honeysuckle hang richly overhead in bowers and arbours.

Let the wild strawberry run, let her follow her imagination.

Let her drape the bank, or base of the towered tree, blooming deliciously.

Bearing her rich ripe berries profusely in the autumn;

Or let the centuried oak display her strength in leaves and acorns;

Or the lofty elm arise to the clouds, pillared and majestic;

Or the sturdy, depending beech stoop gracefully to the brim of the pool, or the meadow;

Or the tall and stately ash raise her arms lightly to the heavens;

Or the fruitful walnut spread the treasury of her leaves with dews and essences;

Or the thick walls of chestnut prepare their gifts of glooms and shadows.

Let the rich harbour his wealth, let the fool covet his inheritance;

Give skill to the artist, let him be big with execution;

To judges dignity and sense; to ambassadors secrecy;

To the trained musician scores of sounds and symphonies;

A ready wit to the pleader, patience to the parliament;

Let the Church think gravely, let her be long-suffering;

Let her continue in hope, and still go forward, there is no end yet;

To-morrow the day will break. To-morrow is eternity. To-morrow the Lord cometh.

To-day we labour, but rest is at hand, we shall soon lie down deeply.

All the joy is of battle, that is the gate of inspiration.

Death is not freely given, we must win immortality.

We must buy our delight, we must bear our toil patiently;

A little of the present will purchase an eternity of future;

Let the workman go to his task cheerfully, and return in the evening;

Let the smith labour in his forge, let the anvils ring out merrily;

Let the furnaces roar and the steam overhead, let the wheels go round;

Let the carpenter, in neat white apron, stand ready with his instruments;

Give him the plane and the square, let him deal in joints and fixtures;

Let the mason ascend the high roof, let him pile the freestone and granite;

Let him chisel the outward feature to appearance, let him rear monuments;

And let the humble tiller of the soil delight in his craft also;

Let him plough faithfully, drawing the deep furrow up and down the headland;

Let him sow in hope, and call Providence down; let the womb of the earth conceive freely for him;

Let the Spring heighten his fancy, let him be rich with expectation;

And let the yellow Autumn load him with joy greater than all words;

Here, in the orchard of life, I will blossom and fall, I will bear my fruit
    in bunches,
I will scatter my seed in the earth, I will leave my world behind me.

IX.

O my beloved! You look strangely at me to-night, you are very still and
    silent.
Many times I called out to you, but you did not answer me.
Your heart is heavy, and mine also; feebly the day dies down, the shade
    arises,
The breath of earth streams with it, slowly the cloud stoops, the air
    perishes;
The hills are hid with vapour, the stars come out overhead, nature's eye
    is shut.
The old pheasant roosts in the tree, I can see him plainly over the pool;
The blackbird sleeps in the bush, the bats circle and wheel, the cattle lie
    down;
The river winds in its course, too full for song; everywhere silence;
Dead, living silence; dull, dreamless silence; soul-shattering silence;
Better the roaring tempest, scattering the fresh raindrops with it,
The bitter breath of the North, the piercing East, or the West victorious.
Than this eternal vacancy of sound, this crystal nothing, body-breaking
    silence.
I have watched the leaves wither and fade, yellow and pale on the edges,
I have seen the red beech fall, the green ash widowed,
The old elms scattering their souls in clouds, the willows and maples.
The young hazels sicken and droop, the berries on the briar ripen,
I have daily plucked the sweet blackberries, I have nursed them to
    maturity,
Before the nipping hoarfrost touched them with his finger, and blew his
    breath over them;
I have watched the old sun stoop lower and lower, and the moon come up
    higher and higher above me;
I have seen the corn gathered and the thresher come forth, I have seen the
    earth ploughed up;

I have seen the seed scattered and the rain falling in torrents, I have seen
the sky come down;

I have seen legions of birds hovering over the bare brown fields, and the
night lengthening;

Everywhere the lesson of death — death, tearful and apprehensive; death,
living and triumphant.

And in my soul the clear testament of death, the strong calm, the silence
and stillness of it.

The bird of thought flown, imagination fettered, reason distracted,

Death in my fingers, the cold slowly creeping up, slowly enveloping;

Then I climbed quickly up to you, I clasped you in my arms, I covered
you with embraces;

I laid my cheek against yours, I cried loudly for deliverance;

I woke from my slumber, I stirred up the pool of thought, I roused you
up also;

I shouted at the top of my voice, I drove away silence, I loosed death from
my fingers,

I would not bear his embraces, I shook him off mightily;

I read in the lesson of death the moral of life returning;

Everywhere hope; in the brown fields, in the dry leaves scattered beneath
my feet,

Light in darkness, day hid in night, strength in weakness;

And in my soul again, like a river welling eternally,

The endless living flood of life, life, life;

The joy of life, the beauty of breathing, the delirium of existence;

The sum of all thought, and the execution of it, dear, living, immortal life.

X.

O Art! O Knowledge! the world's tutor, ancient and scientific;

The universal tree, full of strange fruits, and learned exhibitions,

Ofttimes bitter to the taste, not always sure, and very insufficient;

You have solved many mysteries; you have revealed secrets long hid; you
have shattered idols;

You have reared up cities from the dust, and drawn the maps of empires;

You have carved and chiselled Time, you have counted stars and planets;

You have greatly fathered Thought, you have fed Imagination;
You have made Learning rich, you have divested Ignorance;
You have shattered disputation, you have torn the web of argument;
You have enriched Wisdom, you have strengthened Opinion;
You have encouraged hope in some things, and destroyed it in others;
You have determined causes, you have proved the birth of issues;
You have removed boundaries, and swept away demarcations;
You have drawn the Past's picture, you have brought Antiquity down
     to us;
You have winnowed reigns and periods, you have deciphered monuments;
You have interpreted tongues and signs, you have harvested the fruits of
     labour;
You have immortalized diligence, and perpetuated utility;
You have taught the doctrine of deliverance, you have worshipped truth
     and sanity;
But you have reared other idols, you have your shrines and sanctuaries;
You have your letters and creeds, you are very dogmatical;
Though you teach subjection, you are not humility;
You are a rich servant but a poor master;
Though full of certitude yourself, you fill others with illusion;
You are so full of substance, you cannot see the shadow;
So clamorous for the end, you are lost to the beginning;
In your haste to convince others, you fall a victim to yourself;
Often teaching the remedy of light, you are a prey to blindness.
O the ignorance of knowledge, the vacancy of thought, the folly of
     wisdom!
What are the riches and reward of learning, the pomps and vanities?
There is no learning greater than what teaches me of myself;
And little of high value that will not better humanity.
My reckoning is not with the body, I relegate that duty to others;
I am not the doctor of my kind, there are many physicians.
Whether I be fat or lean, I am still very like and similar;
That is but wasted effort which is spent on a flower ephemeral,
That the first frost of death will fade and wither in a moment.
There is more sweetness in adversity than in all the petals of Fortune;
And more rapture of defeat, than in all the triumphs of victory.

Give them the whip and the spur, that is the balm and the remedy.
Let not Comfort creep in like a thief, it will spoil sincerity.
I must prick my body for blood, and my soul for a sweetness.
While my body is at rest it knows nothing of adventure;
And the soul that slumbers is eternally dead to itself.
I will follow the index of knowledge but unto reconciliation.
That is the goal of my life, to covet hereafter,
And from the nothing I have been to greatly establish myself;
Counting all outward ornament but a hindrance to my happiness;
The God of Nature my hope, knowledge my faculty,
Poorness my wealth, sickness my safety, death my deliverance.

XI.

O if I could lift humanity up, if I could teach them happiness!
If I could persuade them to a hope, or speak strong comfort to them!
If I could dispel the cloud, if I could induce brightness!
If I could improve opinion, and instruct sympathy!
If I could engender love, and compact friendships!
Draw all the earth into one bond, all difference of peoples!
If I could heal all ruptures and wounds, all pains and sufferings;
Pour out the balm of kindness, put an end to bitterness!
Or even stretch out an arm, and draw them gently to myself!
If I were not so feeble, if my breath had utterance,
And they, on their part, would drink at the well of disposition;
I would wipe away all tears, I would wrap them with sunshine;
I would strew flowers in their way, I would give them offerings of roses;
I would make the pure delicious lilies bloom everlasting around them;
I would blot out all difference, I would pillory distinction;
I would put down pride, I would make them sing songs and choruses;
I would lead them through the green walks of life, under trees and
    arbours;
They should draw the breath of Nature, they should pace beside streams
    and waters,
Down the long slopes of hills, yellow with corn, into deep valleys;
They should know the sweetness of woods, they should pitch their tents
    in orchards;

They should see the dear primrose bloom, and the shaded violet;
They should hear the woods ring, and see the fond cattle lying down;
They should wander out under the stars, mute with adoration.
With perfect love in their hearts, strongly knit in affection.
There should be no more wars, wives should cherish husbands,
Mothers rejoice in their sons, maidens fear not for lovers.
The old vows should be breathed, pledges given and accepted,
The crowning happiness of life, the marriages and bridals.
Labour should be reprieved, I would pacify contention;
I would grant freedom to all, the character of fraternity.
Let us give thanks to the present, let us bless opportunity.
Let us live largely to-day. Now the heart beats, now the blood runs
    wildly.
To-morrow the stream is silent, the flood is out, the wind blows drearily.
Time will prove all prophecy; he will bear my word witness;
I look forward bravely, I cherish my hope, I favour fulfilment.

XII.

O my beloved! let us pour out our souls once more finally together.
Down with your branches and leaves, down with your lights and
    shadows,
Stoop low to the earth, this is where I am, bend down over me;
Cover me with your mantle, rock me in your arms, sing me to slumber;
Tell me some story of the past, crown me with hope of the future;
But O let us lovingly rejoice in the present, let us live together;
Let us drink up pleasure, and woo further delight; let us compel happiness;
All day I am broken and bruised, I am very sad and sorrowful.
I have borne the whip and the lash, I am deeply tormented.
I have heard the coward's tongue crying out, thick with reproaches.
I have felt the sting of shame, I have groaned inwardly to myself.
I have hoped against hope; I have walked in glooms and shadows.
I have seen right worsted, wrong many times triumphant.
I have seen the weak oppressed, I have seen cowards stand by poorly.
I have caught the breath of liars, I have heard the mouths of hypocrites.
I have seen the round tear fall, I have read despair writ in faces.

I have seen the fool prosper and pride hoisted up, merit unrewarded.
I know the hollow mockery of power, that unworthy idol.
I have heard the cry go up, my own was always ready to be with it;
Still I stifled it down, I shut it up in my heart firmly;
I sealed the door of my lips, I nursed my grief bravely;
I bore all reproaches, I made peace with complaint, I suffered humiliation.
O cravens and cowards! O blind fools and hypocrites!
You yourselves bear the lash, you are the diseased sufferers.
You are the strong traducers, the pullers down of principals;
The blind barriers to merit, the misinterpreters of government,
The poor perverters of justice, the vile administrators.
I envy no man his wealth, I will not wax rich with flattery.
As for your popular favours, I turn my face contemptuously from them;
I give them back their speeches and emoluments, I am not a beggar.
I could give them more than they have, though I possess nothing,
And still be content with my portion, so fruitful is my poverty.
I am happy with a cottage or without one; the earth is my dwelling.
I can walk bare-headed, and bare-footed, and divest myself,
But I would not raise an arm to my parent, this spot of earth, this mother
    of me.
Nor let my voice be heard in one contumely against her,
Who lovingly brought me forth and carried me in her bosom,
And will one day open her bosom again tenderly to receive me.
Whatever her follies, I forgive them. She has very often wept for me.
She has suffered blood for my sake, she has battled with the enemy;
She has been pierced with wounds, and several times brought near to
    death;
When the foe tormented she kept him out bravely;
Many of her sons, and my brothers, gave themselves up nobly in the
    breach;
She deprived the lips of others to give food for my safety,
And received their deaths calmly for my sake, and others yet to come.
Storing the fruits of her kindness up for me and for many.
And I will not be unnatural in my loving regard for her,
Nor in the greatness of my soul hear one thing spoken unworthily.

Who has been so merciful to us all, and so motherly;
I will not be guilty of so great a fault, I should think myself twice worthy
    of hell;
I will die in my poverty, blessing it and blessing her, I will live for my
    country.

XIII.

This is the date of my song; this is my testament.
In it I have drawn my picture, I have taken note of myself,
I have looked in my own glass, I have studied the book of passions,
I have read states and feelings, I have threshed thought indoors and out,
I have seen myself inwardly, and I have observed at a distance.
And compared myself with others both in and out of season.
I have my follies and foibles, my flesh and blood weaknesses;
I am not the model of my kind, the father of humanity.
I am one with all purpose, I stand ready for improvements,
I am no slave to custom, no deprecator of expedient.
Though I am fanciful, yet I am not a dreamer;
I see the reality of truth through the thin shadow of fiction.
I am the apostle of hope, I am the proof of destiny,
I am the finger of faith, the prophet of deliverance,
The strong prison of pride, the death of hypocrisy.
The scorner of artifice, the bold wrecker of convention.
All life has its recompense, I am not unrewarded;
I am full of strong rumour, I am great with futurity.